Teaching Young Children
With Autism Spectrum Disorder
by Clarissa Willis

Acknowledgments

Special thanks to Miss Beverly and all the wonderful children at the East Tennessee State University Child Study Center, and Miss Cheryl and her staff at the Child Development Center at the University of Southern Mississippi. For your support and expertise, thank you to Sheila P. Smith, my resident editor, and Michael Talley, whose photographs truly capture the wonder of childhood. My staff: Kathy Greer, Helen Lane, Donna Nelson, Roxanne Stanley, and Brandy Sullivan, and finally to my friends who have inspired and believed in this project since the beginning: Rebecca Isbell, Pam Schiller, Sharon MacDonald, and Ann Marie Leonard.

Dedication

This book is dedicated to my husband and best friend, Mike; my daughter Kimberly; and all the children with autism I have been lucky enough to be involved with; you have all taught me more than you will ever know.

Teaching Young Children With Autism Spectrum Disorder

Clarissa Willis

Photographs: Michael Talley

Illustrations: Marie Ferrante Doyle

Sign Language Illustrations: Deborah Johnson

Published by Gryphon House, Inc.
10726 Tucker Street, Beltsville, MD 20705
301.595.9500; 301.595.0051 (fax); 800.638.0928 (toll-free)

Visit us on the web at www.ghbooks.com

Library of Congress Cataloging-in-Publication Data
Willis, Clarissa.
  Teaching young children with autism spectrum disorder / Clarissa Willis ; photographs, Michael Talley ; illustrations, Marie Ferrante Doyle ; sign language illustrations, Deborah Johnson.
    p. cm.
  ISBN-13: 978-0-87659-008-9
  1. Autistic children--Education. 2. Autism in children. I. Title.
  LC4717.W55 2006
  371.94--dc22

                          2006017065

Gryphon House is a member of the Green Press Initiative, a nonprofit program dedicated to supporting publishers in their efforts to reduce their use of fiber sourced forests. For further information visit www.greenpressinitiative .org.

Bulk Purchase
Gryphon House books are available for special premiums and sales promotions as well as for fund-raising use. Special editions or book excerpts also can be created to specification. For details, contact the Director of Marketing at Gryphon House.

Disclaimer
Gryphon House, Inc. and the author cannot be held responsible for damage, mishap, or injury incurred during the use of or because of activities in this book. Appropriate and reasonable caution and adult supervision of children involved in activities and corresponding to the age and capability of each child involved, is recommended at all times. Do not leave children unattended at any time. Observe safety and caution at all times. Every effort has been made to locate copyright and permission information.

Table of Contents

Chapter 3
Planning for Success: Setting Up a Proactive Preschool Environment   43

Chapter 4
Learning Life Skills: What Are Life Skills?   65

Chapter 5
Misbehavior or Missed Communication: Managing the Behaviors of Children With Autism 89

Chapter 6
Signs, Symbols, and Language: Helping a Child Communicate 107

Chapter 7

Inside Their Own Worlds: Encouraging Children With Autism to Play   135

Chapter 8

Building Social Skills: Getting Along With Others   157

Chapter 9
Lights! Camera! Action! Sensory Integration and Autism   179

Chapter 10
We're All in This Together: Teaming Up With Families   197

Introduction

While the other children play in centers in the three- and four-year-old classroom, Gina looks out the window as if she is watching a bird flying across the sky. She stands at the window for 30 minutes, silently wringing her hands, smiling, and humming to herself. During periods of transition, Graham flaps his hands repeatedly and rocks back and forth. He can tell you all the words to his favorite song, but when asked his name, he looks away.

It is lunch time in the pre-k classroom; everyone sits down at the table. Today will be

a challenge, because Darren only eats things that are white and cannot tolerate noise or bright light.

All the children at the preschool are going on a field trip to the grocery store. They will buy food and then prepare their own snacks. While most children look forward to a trip to the store, for Janine, it is a nightmare of sounds, smells, and textures that overload her system and cause her to fall to the floor screaming.

Marcus tolerates other people. In fact, sometimes he will hug his parents when they ask. He already can count to 20, even though he is only four, and his favorite activities are watching the same movie over and over and playing the same video games for hours.

All of these children have varying degrees of Autism Spectrum Disorder, which will affect their behavior, communication skills, ability to relate to others, and, in some cases, their ability to learn in the same way as typically developing children. While there is no cure for autism, there is hope for children like those described here. With structured early intervention, consistent behavior management, and speech and language intervention, many individuals with autism lead productive lives.

Today, many treatments for autism are available. While some of those treatments are controversial, others are based on years of sound scientific research. However, most professionals agree that each child with autism is unique and has his or her own set of strengths and weaknesses, and each child falls somewhere on a spectrum having a few more or a few less of certain characteristics than other children. This book will explain autism in simple terms, discuss the major characteristics associated with autism, and offer some simple strategies for helping children with autism function in a preschool setting.

The following statement sums it up best, "Autism isn't something a person has, or a 'shell' someone is trapped inside. There is no normal child hidden behind the autism…Autism is a way of being" (Jim Sinclair, 1993).

Putting All of the Pieces Together:

Understanding This Puzzle Called Autism

How Is Autism Defined?

Children with autism have been around much longer than the condition known as autism has had an official name. Leo Kanner first defined autism in 1943 when he published a paper describing 11 children with similar characteristics. The following year in Germany, Hans Asperger described a group of older children with behavior issues. Although they had never met, both men used identical terms to describe the disorder.

Putting all the pieces together

The most accepted definition of autism comes from the Diagnostic and Statistical Manual of Mental Disorders, Fourth Edition-Text Revision (DSM-IV-TR). This manual is used by the American Psychological Association to diagnose and identify the characteristics of specific mental and emotional disorders. According to the DSM-IV-TR, to be diagnosed with autism, a person must demonstrate either delayed or atypical behaviors in the following categories:

◆ Interaction with others (social interaction)
◆ Communication (response to others)
◆ Behavior (examples include bizarre or stereotypical behaviors such as hand wringing or rocking back and forth).

The American Autism Society defines autism as "a complex developmental disability that typically appears during the first three years of life."

With new research and information, more is understood about diagnosing and treating autism than ever before. Unfortunately, the more that experts learn about autism, the more they discover what is unknown about this disorder that, according to the National Institutes of Health, may affect as many as 1 in every 500 children.

According to the National Institutes of Health, this disorder may affect as many as 1 in every 500 children.

Today, many children with autism attend regular preschools and child care facilities. Thus, child care providers need to know what they can do to help children with autism reach their full potential. What do you do when a three-year-old with autism falls on the floor kicking and screaming? How do you communicate with a child who looks away and flaps his hands? What do you do with a four-year-old who watches the ceiling fan as it rotates around and around? Whom do you call if you suspect a child in your class has autism?

All children can learn.

Regardless of what definition is used, as you plan for a child with autism to come into your classroom, you will need the following:

◆ up-to-date, accurate information about the primary characteristics of autism;
◆ a strong support system that includes specialists such as early interventionists, special education teachers, speech pathologists, and occupational therapists;
◆ a positive relationship with the child's family so that together you can share the child's successes and challenges.
◆ training in how to help with the child's behavior, communication, social skills, self-help skills, and stereotypical behaviors.

Why Is It Called Autism Spectrum Disorder?

If you were asked to think about a specific child in your classroom and make a list of the things she did well, the things she was just learning to do, and the things she needed to work on, it would seem like a simple task. Some children run faster than others, some are naturally more social, some children love the block area, while others seem enchanted by the dramatic play center.

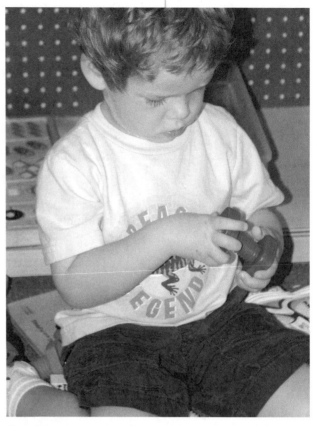
Provide toys the child enjoys.

In a preschool setting, a child's specific strengths usually center on the activities he enjoys because most typically developing children spend more time doing the things that are fun for them and less time doing things that are difficult. Children with autism are the same as other children in that they also have individual preferences and styles. However, those preferences are often expressed in different ways. For example, a child with autism may move, play with toys, or relate to objects differently than her peers. While a typically developing child may take turns rolling a car back and forth with a friend, a child with autism may play only with red cars and instead of rolling the car along the floor, she will turn it over and spin one wheel repeatedly.

Autism is described as a spectrum disorder because children with autism have characteristics that fall into a spectrum from very mild to quite severe. When discussing a child with autism, the existing literature will refer to him as having Autism Spectrum Disorder, or ASD, which means the child falls somewhere along a continuum between very severe and very mild. The child's place on the continuum helps determine how to plan for his education. Because it is a continuum, a child may be at the mild end in terms of ability to learn new skills, and at the severe end in terms of behavior around other children. Generally, a single child is described as having an autism spectrum disorder, and a group of children are described as having autism spectrum disorders. For the purposes of this book, the term *autism* refers to a child who has an autism spectrum disorder.

While each child with autism is unique, it is generally agreed that all children with autism spectrum disorders have difficulty in varying levels of:
◆ language and communication,
◆ social relationships, and
◆ response to sensory stimuli.

Children with autism are the same as other children in that they also have individual preferences and styles. However, those preferences are often expressed in different ways.

In addition, these children usually will display behaviors that are not typical of their peers. For example, many young children with autism have gaps in their development ranging from learning skills out of sequence to fixation on objects such as a puzzle or a rotating fan. Teachers often describe a child with autism as being like a piece of Swiss cheese—there are gaps or holes in what they learn, how they learn it, and how they respond to their world.

Before discussing what autism is, it is important to look at some myths about autism that persist, including:

♦ **Autism is contagious.** While there is research showing that autism sometimes runs in families, it is not contagious. Children cannot catch it from each other like they catch a cold.

♦ **Autism only affects boys.** Even though it is four times more common in males than in females, autism affects both genders.

♦ **Autism is caused by aloof parents who are emotionally unresponsive.** Bad or inattentive parenting does not cause autism.

♦ **Children with autism are always mean and hurt others.** Children with autism are not always aggressive and mean. In fact, many children with autism are very timid and, if anything, are more likely to hit or hurt themselves than they are to harm others.

♦ **Children with autism never learn to communicate and play with other children.** Communication is often difficult for children with autism, and many children learn alternative ways to communicate and play. However, most children with autism can learn to communicate.

♦ **Children with autism are always unhappy and cry a lot.** While crying and tantrums are seen in children with autism, they can be controlled and, in some cases, can be stopped all together.

♦ **Children with autism live in their own worlds all the time.** Obsession with objects and movement is often seen in children with autism. However, when engaged and involved in an activity, they often interact and respond like other children.

♦ **Children with autism don't like to be touched.** Tactile sensitivity is common in children with autism. However, many children enjoy a hug and being close to the people in their worlds.

♦ **All children with autism have genius-like talents, such as playing the piano or solving mathematical equations.** Highly-developed talents at a young age are present in a small number of children with autism and are not seen in most children with autism.

♦ **Children with autism die young.** Left untreated, a child with autism will never reach his full potential. However, autism is not a degenerative condition; it will not get worse as the child grows older. In fact, the opposite is true. Many people with autism learn to function better as they grow older.

> *Teachers often describe a child with autism as being like a piece of Swiss cheese—there are gaps or holes in what they learn, how they learn it, and how they respond to their world.*

Words, Words, Words—Why Is There So Much Autism-Related Jargon?

It is often very confusing to read about autism, because of all the terms associated with it. With all the responsibilities that go with teaching young children, the last thing a teacher needs is to be saddled with a dictionary to learn about a child's condition. For example, a speech pathologist tells the teacher in a classroom full of three-year-olds that a young boy with autism needs to stop using *echolalia* and learn to use functional communication. After searching the Internet to decipher what the speech pathologist was referring to, the teacher learns that echolalia is a term that simply means repeating everything that is heard.

This book will help to explain autism, as it relates to young children, without using jargon. When a specific term is used, it will be explained in simple terms. Definitions of key terms are provided at the end of each chapter, and most chapters include specific strategies or activities that you can use in your classroom. Most of these activities take very little time and cost almost nothing to make. It is important that as you try to understand a child with autism, you view him as a special and unique person with talents, strengths, and potential. These reminders focus on what the child can learn, rather than what can't be learned.

◆ **Always put the child first.** He is a child with autism, not an autistic child. Also, remember that he has a name and should be called by his name as much and as often as possible.

- **Each child is unique,** and while she may have characteristics typical of other children with autism, she will have other characteristics that are not.
- **Look for information about autism from a reliable source and remember that there may be more than one way to solve an autism-related problem.** Information, even what is seen or heard on television and the Internet, may not come from reliable sources.
- **There is no single method, magic pill, or specific program that can cure or fix autism.** While many programs and methods have been tried and are successful with some children, they may not be successful with others. If a method seems too good to be true or promises a cure for autism, chances are that it is being presented by someone wanting to sell a product. That product may or may not be backed by sound research. Parents are often the targets of people trying to sell expensive products or methods related to autism.
- **Learning about autism is not about a product;** it is about a process of gathering information and making informed choices based on the needs of the individual child. The National Autism Center, a nonprofit organization dedicated to dissemination of information about autism, is attempting to develop a comprehensive autism clearinghouse, which includes a database of information about autism. Once in place, the system will allow professionals to work together and share information with each other.

Interacting with peers

What Are the Major Types of Autism?

DSM-IV-TR classifies autism-related disorders into a single broad category referred to as Pervasive Developmental Delay (PDD). The terms Pervasive Developmental Delay and Autism Spectrum Disorder (ASD) are sometimes used interchangeably in the current literature, and essentially they have the same meaning. One analogy is to think of PDD/ASD as a tree with several branches growing from the same trunk. Each branch, though slightly different from the other branches, is still part of the tree. The same is true of the various types of autism.

The recognized types of autism spectrum disorder include:
- Autism
- Pervasive Developmental Disorder Not Otherwise Specified (PDDNOS)
- Asperger's Syndrome

- Rett's Syndrome
- Childhood Disintegrative Disorder (Heller's Syndrome)

Autism

To be diagnosed with autism, a child must exhibit a significant number of the following characteristics:
- a significant delay in social interaction, such as eye contact or facial expression
- a communication delay
- behaviors including stereotypical behavior, such as intense, almost obsessive, preoccupation with objects
- the need for routines that are non-functional and ritualistic, such as lining up all the books or food in a certain manner
- repeating motor movements over and over, such as finger-popping or hand-flapping

Pervasive Developmental Disorder Not Otherwise Specified (PDDNOS)

This classification is used when it is determined that a child has autism, although the characteristics displayed by the child are not like the characteristics of other children with autism. This diagnosis is also used when the onset of the disorder happens after age three. Of all the classifications used for autism, this is the most vague and confusing for both parents and teachers. However, this classification allows a child with a few, but not all, of the characteristics of autism to be classified as having autism so that he can receive the needed services.

Asperger's Syndrome

Children with Asperger's Syndrome traditionally behave much like children with other types of autism when they are young, in that they will have some difficulty with communication, social interaction, and/or behaviors. However, as they grow into middle school age or in adolescence, they often learn how to socialize, communicate, and behave in a more socially acceptable manner. Most children with Asperger's have normal or above normal intelligence, so they learn new skills as fast or, in many cases, faster than their peers without autism. These children have been described as having difficulty with coordination, vocal tone (they tend to speak in a monotone), depression, violent reactions to change, and they have a tendency for ritualistic behaviors. In addition, children with Asperger's Syndrome may develop intense obsessions with objects or activities. Unlike other children with ASD, these children tend to develop normally in the areas of self-help and adaptive behaviors, with the only exception appearing in the area of social skills, which is often delayed.

Rett's Syndrome

Also referred to as Rett's Disorder, this is a degenerative disability, meaning it gets worse with time. It begins sometime in the first two years of life and is found almost exclusively in girls. Unlike other types of autism, children with Rett's Syndrome develop normally prior to the onset of the disorder. Characteristics include loss of motor skills, hand-wringing or repetitive hand washing, and a decrease in head growth. Seizures and sleeping disorders also develop in many girls with this disorder.

Childhood Disintegrative Disorder

This disorder, sometimes called Heller's Syndrome, is a degenerative condition in which a child may begin to develop normally, but, over a few months, will begin to lose the ability or seem to forget how to do things. It usually happens in the areas of toilet training, play skills, language, or problem-solving. This degeneration or loss of skills usually happens between ages three and four.

When and How Is Autism Diagnosed?

Some children with autism are diagnosed by the time they are two years of age. For others, the symptoms are not recognized until they are older. Autism is, however, a medical diagnosis and requires a full examination by a qualified physician. The medical evaluation may be completed by a pediatrician, psychiatrist, or a team of medical providers. This evaluation will determine if the child meets the medical or psychological criteria for autism. While many physicians are hesitant to diagnose a child younger than two, there are benefits to an early diagnosis. The sooner a child starts receiving treatment, the better his prognosis is likely to be.

A second evaluation, given by educational personnel will determine if the child is eligible for services, such as early intervention services or speech therapy. Most states provide services to children with special needs from birth through age 21. However, each state has its own criteria for eligibility.

How Do I Know What Services Are Available for Children With Autism?

Once a child has been diagnosed with autism, there are laws that help determine what services she is entitled to receive. The Individuals With Disabilities Education Act (IDEA) (Public Law 101-476) outlines very specific guidelines that local school districts are required by law to adhere to when providing for the needs of children with disabilities.

For children age 3-21 with disabilities:

◆ Each school district must provide a Free and Appropriate Public Education (FAPE). This includes all aspects of special education such as speech therapy, occupational therapy, and transportation. In addition, these services must be provided without cost to parents. Not all children with disabilities qualify for all services. Many school districts do not have programs for three-year-olds, so they may choose to contract with outside child care providers or centers where typically developing children may be enrolled.

◆ Assessments must be non-biased and non-discriminatory. They must be conducted in the child's native language, and, most importantly, educational decisions about a child cannot be made based on a single test. In other words, a variety of assessments are used to determine eligibility for educational services.

◆ Once a child has been determined as eligible for services, an educational plan is developed and written by a team that includes the child's family. This team reviews and updates the Individual Education Plan (IEP) each year. The child's IEP clearly outlines what types of service he will receive and how often he will receive the service.

◆ The child must receive the service to which she is entitled in an environment that is the least restrictive. It is presumed, and was made clear in the most recent reauthorization of IDEA, that the least restrictive environment should be the general education classroom, unless there are justifications why it would not be appropriate. Many school districts elect to contract with a private preschool to provide these services.

Children from birth to age three with autism usually receive services through a state-provided comprehensive early intervention system. The child is assigned a service coordinator who works with the family to assess the child, plan appropriate services, and develop an Individual Family Service Plan (IFSP). The IFSP is a written plan for services the child will receive, and it helps guide the family as the child transitions into other programs. For children from birth to age three, services are provided in the child's natural environment. The natural environment is defined as the place where the

The natural environment may be a preschool.

child might spend time if she did not have a disability. In most cases, the natural environment is at home. However, if both parents work, the natural environment may be a school, child care center, or a private home child care provider.

What Are the Most Common Treatments for Autism?

It can be overwhelming when a child with autism is placed in your care. With so many treatments for autism, how can anyone know which one works best? Some treatments claim that certain diets or vitamins will help children with autism behave more normally. In addition, addressing the issues related to sensory integration disorder, such as sensitivity to noise or smell, has also allowed many children with autism to function better in a preschool setting. Table 1-1 contains a list of the types of services that children with autism might receive.

Table 1-1: Services for Children With Autism*

Treatment	Definition
Structured Behavior Intervention	A plan to help the child manage his behavior designed by a specialist trained in applied behavior analysis (ABA).
Early Intervention	Services, usually home-based, which are provided for the child through a special education teacher. This is usually used to describe services received before the child is three years old.
Sensory Integration Therapy	Usually implemented by an occupational therapist, designed to help the child handle all input received from his environment.
Speech/Language Therapy	A speech language pathologist works with the child to facilitate communication and language.
Special Education	The special education teacher is responsible for implementing the child's Individual Education Plan (IEP) and for working with the classroom teacher to help the child reach his full potential.

*   Before implementing any treatment, please consult a qualified professional such as the child's physician, speech pathologist, or special education teacher.

As a Preschool Teacher, What Do I Need to Know About Children With Autism?

The most important thing teachers need to know is that the sooner a child with autism receives sound, consistent, and appropriate services, the better his chance for success. While there is still much to learn about how to reach children with autism and how to help them adapt to a world that is constantly changing, we know that working with parents and other professionals can lead to positive results.

Despite all that is known, there is still much to learn about autism and its effects on children. However, experts do agree on two things: Autism cannot be cured, and there is no plan or program that will completely eliminate all of the characteristics of the disorder. Programs addressing the characteristics of autism while combining the medical and educational needs of the child are most effective.

Most professionals working with children with autism agree that successful programs combine sound, structured educational programming with developmentally appropriate practices. To help a child with autism maximize his potential, it is critical for families to play an important decision-making role in planning for the education of their child. Today, scientists from major research universities, such as Harvard, Vanderbilt, and Johns Hopkins, are exploring what happens inside the brain of a child with autism. Using modern technology, such as Positron Emission Tomography (PET), researchers are, for the first time, able to look at the electrical energy within the brain to determine what part of the brain is responsible for certain actions and behaviors.

To help a child with autism maximize his potential, it is critical for families to play an important decision-making role in planning for the education of their child.

Increasingly, these researchers are finding evidence of a disruption or change in the brains of children with autism that is not seen in their typically developing peers. Other scientists are finding that in the brain of a child with autism, serotonin is broken down and used differently. In simple terms, in the brain of a typically developing child, connections are made between brain cells. Much like a computer takes in and puts out data, these connections carry information among the parts of the brain and between other parts of the body and the brain. In children with autism, these pathways, or information connections, within the brain are made differently. This could explain why children with autism often respond to sensory input so differently than their peers.

Gastroenterologists (stomach specialists) who specialize in children with autism have begun to closely examine the relationship between the brain and the child's overall physical health. They are specifically trying to determine if certain behaviors related to autism, such as hand flapping, are caused to some degree

Developmentally
appropriate activity

by stomach conditions, such as constipation or bladder infections. Medical specialists now recognize that there are times when children with autism have a physical illness that contributes to their tantrums or violent behavior.

While research hopefully will lead to new and better techniques for working with children with autism, for now, teachers want to know what to do with a child who has autism, how to help the child control his behavior, and what programs or plans work best so the child can learn to communicate, play, and interact meaningfully with peers. This book is designed to help preschool teachers understand autism and enable them to plan for the success of all children, especially those with autism spectrum disorder. Children with autism spectrum disorder display a range of behaviors and abilities from very mild to quite severe. In other words, the term autism can describe a child who fits anywhere within that range. Therefore, for the purposes of this book, *autism* will be used to describe all children within that spectrum. The first step in the planning process is to examine more closely the characteristics seen in a young child with autism and learn how that child relates to the world around him.

Resources Used in This Chapter

Buie, Timothy. 2005. *Treating autism in children: Neuro-gastroenterology and autism.* A paper presented at Harvard University: Learning and the Brain Conference (12th Conference), Cambridge, MA.

Janzen, J. E. 2003. *Understanding the nature of autism: A guide to the autism spectrum disorders.* San Antonio, TX: Therapy Skill Builders.

Kluth, P. 2003. *You're going to love this kid!: Teaching students with autism in the inclusive classroom.* Baltimore, MD: Paul H. Brookes Publishing Co.

Murray-Slutsky, C. & B.A. Paris. 2001. *Exploring the spectrum of autism and pervasive developmental disorders: Intervention strategies.* New York: Elsevier Science.

Sicile-Kira, C. 2004. *Autism spectrum disorders: The complete guide to understanding autism, Asperger's Syndrome, pervasive developmental disorder, and other ASDs.* New York: The Berkley Publishing Group.

Sigman, M.& L. Capps. 1997. *Children with autism: A developmental perspective.* Cambridge, MA: Harvard University Press.

Sinclair, J. 1993. Don't mourn for us. *Autism Network International Newsletter,* 1(3).

Weatherby, A.M., & B. Prizant. 2001. *Autism spectrum disorders: A transactional developmental perspective,* Vol. 9. Baltimore, MD: Paul H. Brookes Publishing Co.

Key Terms

Autism: A complex developmental disability that typically appears during the first three years of life. To be diagnosed with autism, a person must demonstrate either delayed or atypical behaviors in at least one of three categories: interaction, communication, or behavior.

Autism Spectrum Disorder (ASD): Autism Spectrum Disorder (ASD) is a broad term which includes the classical form of autism as well as several related disabilities that share many of the same characteristics including difficulty with communication, socialization, and behavior. It is called spectrum because autism and autism-related characteristics range from very mild to very severe.

Developmentally appropriate practices: Activities and educational experiences that match the child's age and stage of development.

Echolalia: The echoing and repetition of a phrase or word.

Free and Appropriate Public Education (FAPE): Special education law is clear that a child with disabilities is entitled to an education that is free and appropriate for his individual needs.

Individual Education Plan (IEP): A personalized plan for a child designed by a team, including the child's parents, which outlines the educational goals and objectives for the child over a period of time (usually one school year).

Individual Family Service Plan (IFSP): A written plan for services a child will receive, to help guide the family as the child transitions into other programs. The IFSP is written for children birth to three. Once a child turns three, an IEP is written if he still qualifies for special education services.

Individuals With Disabilities Education Act (IDEA): (Public Law 101-476) IDEA outlines very specific guidelines that local school districts are required by law to adhere to when providing for the needs of children with disabilities.

Least restrictive environment: Under the IDEA all children who require special education services must be educated in the setting that is most appropriate to their individual needs.

Natural environment: The place where the child might spend most of her time if she did not have a disability.

Positron Emission Tomography (PET): Medical testing that looks at the electrical energy within the brain to determine what part of the brain is responsible for certain actions and behaviors.

Ritualistic: Following a set pattern or routine without variation.

Serotonin: A hormone found in the brain. It acts as a chemical messenger that transmits signals between nerve cells. Changes in the serotonin levels in the brain can affect mood and behavior. Serotonin is also found in blood platelets and the digestive tract.

Typically developing: A child who is developing at a rate similar to his peers; a term often used to describe a child without disabilities.

From
Hand Flapping
to Obsession
With Routines:
The Way Children With Autism Relate to Their Worlds

What Can I Expect a Preschool Child With Autism to Do?

Generally, children with autism will have varying levels of difficulty in one or more of the following areas:

- ◆ Maladaptive behaviors or behaviors not typical of their peers
- ◆ Stereotypic behaviors
- ◆ Self-injurious behaviors
- ◆ Obsessions
- ◆ Rituals
- ◆ Tantrums
- ◆ Aggression toward others

Certain behaviors are expressions of anxiety or anger.

- ◆ Language and communication
- ◆ Developing social relationships—especially with peers
- ◆ Responses to noise, smell, light, or other sensory stimuli
- ◆ Self-help or life skills, such as going to the bathroom or washing their hands
- ◆ Medical problems due to poor eating habits or the inability to let someone know when they are hurt or sick

What Exactly Is Maladaptive Behavior?

By definition, maladaptive behavior is a behavior that is not common in most children or a behavior that is so severe that it interferes with learning. Some maladaptive behaviors that children with autism might have include:

- ◆ stereotypic behavior, such as repetitive hand flapping or saying the same phrase repeatedly;
- ◆ behaviors that are self-injurious, such as hitting or biting themselves;
- ◆ obsession with objects, such as collecting forks or watching the blades of a rotating ceiling fan;
- ◆ following rituals, such as only walking on the floor instead of carpet or having to arrange food in a certain order;
- ◆ tantrums beyond those normally seen in children; and
- ◆ over-aggressiveness toward other children, such as hair pulling or biting.

What Is a Stereotypic Behavior?

Stereotypic behavior is usually defined as a behavior that is carried out repeatedly and involves either movement of the child's body or movement of an object. Some of the most common stereotypic behaviors seen in young children with autism include flapping one or both hands, pulling or tapping the ears, rocking back and forth or from side to side, sniffing the air, or sucking on the upper lip. One theory about these behaviors is that children may use these behaviors to "tune out" the world around them because they find certain noises over-stimulating. That is, the behavior gives them internal pleasure and helps them deal with the overwhelming influences of light, sound, and smell. Another, opposite theory is that the child does these behaviors because she is under-stimulated and the stereotypic behaviors increase stimulation.

Stereotypic behavior may be a way the child calms herself. As she soothes herself by moving or rocking, her brain releases a chemical called beta-endorphin. Beta-endorphins help the body calm down and relax. Another possibility that is supported by research is that stereotypic behaviors may be a way children with autism communicate with adults and other children to control their environments. This is especially true when the child has limited or no language. When a child does these stereotypic behaviors, it may elicit attention or interaction from a parent or teacher. The parent or teacher then attends to the child or tries to stop her from doing this unusual behavior. Over time, the child uses the stereotypic behavior to get attention. Using stereotypic behavior as a way of communicating with others may interfere with more appropriate development of language and communication.

Stereotypic behavior is not usually harmful in itself. However, it often interferes with a child's ability to focus on what is going on around her. Occasionally, all children tune out activities they want to avoid. Even very young children will pretend not to hear when told it is time to stop playing. However, unlike typically developing children, children with autism learn that by doing a specific thing, such as rocking their body from side to side, they can temporarily tune out everything around them; it allows them to move further and further into their own world and further and further away from reality.

Why Would a Child Want to Injure Herself?

Injuring oneself on purpose, or self-injurious behavior, is very different from stereotypic behavior. While a child may use stereotypic behavior to soothe herself, or when she is happy, the same child may hit herself repeatedly when she wants to avoid a specific activity or to get something that she wants. Self-injurious behavior is something a child does to hurt herself in an effort to get out of a situation or an environment that is overwhelming. Self-injurious behaviors include:

◆ biting
◆ scratching (the most common places are the hand or the top of the head)
◆ head banging
◆ squeezing parts of the body, until they bruise
◆ pinching parts of the body (usually the arm or hand)

Some experts believe these behaviors occur when a child is sick, such as when she has an ear infection. Other researchers feel that self-injury is a type of seizure over which the child has no control. Regardless of why it happens, self-injurious behaviors must be stopped immediately. Although it is rare, some self-injurious behaviors can cause permanent damage. Whenever a child starts to injure herself, it is very important that the teacher do whatever is necessary to stop the behavior as quickly as possible. For this reason, it is a good idea to have a plan of action already in place. Perhaps the assistant teacher could remove the other children in the class for a few minutes while the teacher helps the child with autism calm down. A special quiet area in the room where the teacher and child with autism can go together is also helpful if the child begins an activity that might cause her to injure herself. This area should have dim, indirect light, and a comfortable place to sit. The quiet area should never be

Using stereotypic behavior as a way of communicating with others may interfere with more appropriate development of language and communication.

A quiet area is essential.

used as a time-out or punishment area; it is available for the child to relax and escape the sensory overload she is experiencing.

Why Do Children With Autism Become Obsessed With Objects?

It is natural for a young child to be attached to an object, such as a blanket or a favorite toy. This attachment helps the child feel comfortable in new environments. Sometimes, when her favorite toy is nearby it helps her to cope with all the stress of dealing with other people. Most children outgrow the attachment as they grow more social and learn how to express their feelings and desires. Children with autism often develop attachments to objects or toys in a very different way than other children. For example, a child with autism may develop an attachment to a spoon, a rock, or even the round lid of a peanut butter jar. Their attachments tend to be associated with items or objects to which their peers would not become attached.

Unlike other children, who forget about their favorite toy or blanket as soon as something new and novel gets their attention, children with autism remain obsessed with their object for hours, days, or even years. In addition, the object of the obsession usually serves no functional purpose. For example, Tammy enjoys her red car because she can make it go fast on the road she built with her blocks, but as soon as she gets to preschool and sees other types of cars and trucks, she forgets about her red car and plays with the new toys. In contrast, Jill, a child with autism, might be obsessed with a specific red car because she can make the left front wheel spin around repeatedly. Jill will spend a long time spinning the left front wheel over and over. When Jill gets to preschool, she will only play with that red car (the object of her obsession) and she will only spin the left front wheel. Regardless of what other toys are introduced, Jill will only play with one particular red car and, then, only with a specific part of the red car.

Why Do Children With Autism Follow Rituals?

No one really knows why children with autism seem compelled to follow rituals. These rituals may involve an everyday activity, such as brushing teeth or washing hands. They may include things like placing all the blocks in a certain order, getting upset when books on a shelf are not arranged by size, or if a page in a favorite book is bent. Regardless of what the ritual is, it can become very disruptive in the preschool classroom. Some rituals become compulsive, which means the child will perform them repeatedly, stopping, and beginning again, if a certain step is not performed exactly the same way every time. Some researchers feel that these rituals are the child's attempt to control a world that, to her, seems out of control. Others feel it is due to the lack of a chemical in the brain called serotonin. When a child is carrying out one of these rituals, she will seem to be indifferent to the world around her and will often get very upset if this ritual or routine is interrupted for any reason.

When Does a Typical Tantrum Become an Autism-Related Tantrum?

Most preschool teachers can describe what a typical two-year-old tantrum looks like. The tantrums that children with autism have are very much like those of their typically developing peers, with one exception. Typically developing children usually start to outgrow their tantrums by the time they are in preschool and/or they can be distracted by other activities, while children with autism display tantrums much more violently, much longer, and with much more energy than other children. The root cause of the tantrum may be too much environmental stimulation, such as too many sounds. These tantrums may also be triggered by things such as changes in a child's typical routine, changes in her physical environment (a parent rearranges toys in her room while cleaning), or the absence of usual or familiar people (the child's teacher is replaced by a substitute). Another theory is that a tantrum happens when a child with autism goes into sensory overload.

Regardless of the cause, the tantrum is the child's attempt to convey that she is upset, unhappy, frustrated, and anxious about something. Remember, many young children with autism do not communicate their wants and needs like other children, so they may have no other way to let you know they are upset. Once a child with autism has reached the full-blown tantrum stage, there is little, if anything, for you to do but try to keep the child from hurting herself or others. For that reason, the best way to handle a child with autism who has tantrums is to prevent the tantrum by learning what events or actions cause it to occur. It is always good to remember that being proactive (preventing) is much easier than being reactive!

What Is Aggressive Behavior and How Do I Handle It?

Aggressive behavior is behavior that is harmful to others, such as biting, hitting, slapping, kicking, pinching, or pulling hair. Many children with autism are never aggressive toward others. However, when a child is overly tired or overly

Some researchers feel that these rituals are the child's attempt to control a world that, to her, seems out of control. Others feel it is due to the lack of a chemical in the brain called serotonin.

stimulated her only way to protest is to strike what is nearest to her. Aggressive behavior sometimes occurs because it is at least temporarily effective in allowing the child to get something she wants (a favorite toy that another child has) or it allows the child to escape or avoid something she doesn't like (the child becomes aggressive to the parent during bath time and the parent cuts the bath short).

Often, when a child with autism is aggressive toward others, it is because she is communicating a message that her stress level is too high. What the child is really saying in the only way she knows how is, "HELP! STOP! NO!" (For more in-depth information on behavior strategies, see Chapter 5.)

How Do I Know What a Child With Autism Is Trying to Communicate With Her Behavior?

It is very difficult when the teacher does not know what a child is trying to communicate. As the child's frustration at what is going on around her increases, so does the teacher's frustration. (For more in-depth information on communication strategies, see Chapter 6.)

When you do not understand what the child is trying to say to you through her behavior, ask yourself the following questions:

What was the child doing immediately before the behavior started? For example, if Aaron was sitting down for small group time and suddenly stands up and begins to scream, examine what happened immediately before the outburst. Perhaps, you stopped interacting with Aaron, and began talking to the group. If tantrums tend to occur during group activities, it may indicate that Aaron is using the tantrum to regain your attention.

What in the environment might have triggered the outburst or tantrum? Did something make a loud noise? Did it suddenly get brighter in the classroom? Is there a new smell that is unfamiliar to the child? Let's look at another example. Every time the bell rings, signaling the end of the school day, Maria screams. Once the teacher recognizes this, she can give Maria headphones to wear when the bell rings.

What is the child trying to say by her behavior? Remember, sometimes a child will act a certain way to protest, while other times she may cry out as a way of saying, "I don't want to stop yet!" or "There's too much going on here, I can't think!" One key to the purpose or function of a child's behavior is to look at what may consistently (typically) happen after the child's behavior. If the child's tantrum is often followed by some kind of interaction with the adult (even if

Often, when a child with autism is aggressive toward others, it is because she is communicating a message that her stress level is too high.

that attention or interaction appears negative), it may be that the child is communicating (in a maladaptive way) that she wants that person's attention.

Is there something I can do to predict when the child will behave in a certain way? The behaviors of children with autism are not always predictable. However, sometimes knowing what will happen next can prevent an outburst. If Candice starts biting herself every day after you come inside from the playground, it is safe to assume that she found something enjoyable outside and does not want to come inside. Based on this observation, you can cue her with a sign or special signal, right before it is time to come inside. This gives the child time to prepare herself for stopping what she enjoys and helps her prepare to come inside.

Many children with autism learn to talk, while others remain nonverbal. However, just because a child does not talk, it does not mean she cannot learn to communicate. There are several alternative or augmentative forms of communication that children with autism can use. These include:

♦ Sign language: Children with autism can use the same signs used by people who are deaf.
♦ Communication pictures: These are pictures that the child points to when she wants to tell what is happening or what she needs or wants.
♦ Communication devices: Computer-like devices that speak for the child and are activated when he pushes a button or selects a picture.

For more information about communication, see Chapter 6, for descriptions of how children with autism communicate and strategies for helping children communicate more effectively.

Interaction builds social skills.

What Do I Do When a Child Won't Interact With Others?

Whether it is making eye contact or looking at someone when they speak, it is safe to say that most children with autism do not interact with other people the same as their typically developing peers. The ability to interact varies with each child, and some children with Asperger's Syndrome learn to fake it at a very young age. In other words, they learn that if they pretend to attend to a person, or minimally interact by saying, "Hi," or waving goodbye, then people will leave them alone. However, for the most part, children with autism do not start or initiate interactions and often will do almost anything to avoid having to interact with someone. For this reason, social skills training and learning how to respond in social situations should begin as early as possible and should be an ongoing goal throughout the child's education.

It is important to remember to work with the child's parents and other caregivers to prioritize the order in which social skills are taught, as trying to teach the child too many new skills without enough time for practice can be overwhelming. The result may be that the child becomes more withdrawn and is more likely to exhibit a maladaptive behavior in social situations. There are strategies teachers can use to encourage social interaction that are discussed in detail in Chapter 8.

Why Do Children With Autism Have Difficulty With Sensory Stimuli?

Children learn very early how to respond to their environment by using their senses. When only a few months old, a baby learns to recognize her mother by her smell or the sound of her voice. We have all seen a child smack her lips when she smells a favorite food. When something is too loud, a toddler puts her hands over her ears as a signal to "turn down the noise." Unfortunately, unlike other children, children with autism are not able to filter out and respond to information

Holding a favorite toy helps a child stay focused.

that they receive through their senses. To a child with autism, a florescent overhead light, commonly found in most preschool classrooms, can often have the same effect that a powerful flashing strobe light might have on a typically developing child. In addition, the soft ticking of a clock or the hum of a computer might sound entirely different to a child with autism.

Children typically love to touch new objects. The common feely box that many teachers use to introduce new textures is torture to a child with autism. In other words, for a typically developing child, her body is much like a computer in that it is a sensory processing machine. By the time a child is two or three, she learns how to filter sound and how to ignore unimportant sounds in the background. For children with autism, the information they receive from their environment becomes distorted and is not reliable. For this reason, most children with autism have some form of sensory integration disorder. That means they cannot filter or screen out sensory related things. Sensory integration is discussed more completely in Chapter 8.

Can Children With Autism Learn Basic Problem Solving?

Children with autism are similar to their peers in that they have varying degrees of problem-solving skills. Do not assume that a child with autism is cognitively impaired or delayed. While some children with autism perform much like children with developmental delays,

Children learn best when they are relaxed.

many do not. In fact, there are children with autism who are quite skilled at solving complex problems, and will go to great lengths to work out a solution to a difficult problem.

When trying to teach a new skill or a problem-solving task, it is best to keep in mind the following:
- Just like other children, a child with autism learns best when she is rested and relaxed.
- Because change is so difficult, tell the child when you begin to teach her something new. If possible, show her a picture of what she will be doing.
- Introduce a new skill in small segments and provide the child multiple opportunities to practice.
- Most children with autism have difficulty with generalization. That means that while they may be able to perform a skill in one setting or with one

person, they may not be able to do the same task in another environment or with someone who is unfamiliar to them.

◆ Most importantly, children with autism can and do learn new tasks and skills. However, they may learn them in a way that is unique.

Why Do Children With Autism Only Eat Certain Foods?

Sometimes, children with autism will only eat certain foods. For example, they may only eat pizza with cheese or only eat orange gelatin. Often, this obsession with certain foods lasts a lifetime, while sometimes it is temporary. The term used to describe this obsession is called a *food jag*. Some food jags are preferential, meaning that, while they prefer one food over other foods, the child will eat non-preferred foods. Other children are more absolute in their diet, meaning they will only eat certain foods to the exclusion of all others. This type of eating behavior creates challenges at home and at school.

Beyond the obvious problems associated with poor eating habits, such as lack of proper nutrition and variety in the diet, health issues also are involved. Many children with autism have difficulty with chronic diarrhea, constipation, yeast infections, and gas. These stomach problems may or may not be directly related to their diet. However, it is safe to assume, especially if the child eats only a few select foods, that the stomach problems are related.

How Do I Know If a Child With Autism Is Sick?

While we as teachers are not supposed to diagnose or treat the physical illnesses of the children in our class, we should alert parents when we suspect that a child is sick or hurting. Autism-related behaviors could mask when a child is ill. For example, Rebecca, a three-year-old in the class, is usually very social and outgoing. Today, instead of going to the creative activity center (her personal favorite), she goes to the back of the room, lies on the floor, and closes her eyes, or, during small group time, Rebecca puts her hands over her ears and lays her head on the table.

What would you do? The answer is easy. The observant teacher would recognize that something is wrong and that Rebecca is not feeling well. In fact, you might ask, "Rebecca, do your ears hurt? or "Do you feel okay?" You would send her to the nurse to see if she was sick. In addition, when Rebecca's mother comes to pick her up, you would tell her that you suspect Rebecca may be getting sick. However, for a child with autism, you have no way to know how she is feeling, what is hurting, and more importantly, whether something is hurting today that did not hurt yesterday.

While it is challenging and difficult, try to remember that children with autism get sick and need medical attention as much as their typically developing peers; they often do not receive it because their autism interferes with the child getting an accurate diagnosis. For example, Mary hits herself and is prone to violent tantrums. Every time her mother takes her to the pediatrician, she has a violent tantrum and begins to hit herself repeatedly. Because of these behaviors, it may be very difficult for the pediatrician to diagnose a stomach problem. Mary not only cannot tell the doctor where she hurts (gas pains in the stomach), the doctor also cannot get close enough to examine her stomach, because Mary is hitting and screaming. If it were less difficult for the doctor to examine her, it would be easier to see that Mary has issues with gas. Medication might ease her gas pains, thus reducing her tantrums and hitting. Being more aware of the possibility that the child may be in pain or physically ill is the first step to being more responsive to the child and less responsive to the autism itself.

Being more aware of the possibility that the child may be in pain or physically ill is the first step to being more responsive to the child and less responsive to the autism itself.

What About Special Diets?

Some research has been conducted on the effect of gluten and casein on children with autism. Results have shown that the inability to break down certain foods may affect neurological processes in some children, causing behaviors associated with autism. Gluten and casein are proteins found in food that contains wheat, rye, oats, barley, and dairy products. The child's physician can perform a simple Urinary Peptide Test, which detects any protein that is not fully broken down and digested. The decision to remove gluten and casein from a child's diet should always be made by the child's physician.

How Do I Assess a Child With Autism?

While medical personnel and behavior specialists are responsible for assessing a child for the purpose of diagnosis, teachers typically assess for other reasons. For example, a teacher may assess a child with autism to determine her progress in an educational setting or to help decide how to plan goals and objectives appropriate for her age and stage of development. As might be expected, children with autism do not score well on standard early childhood normative checklists. In addition, many tests designed to determine developmental milestones or specific educational standards rely heavily on the child's ability to communicate with the examiner.

Because the objective of an assessment is to demonstrate a child's gain across time, the best form of assessment for a child with autism is a portfolio. Portfolios are collections of the child's work over a specific period and are not

Top: Sample portfolio
Bottom: Sample anecdotal record

intended to be giant scrapbooks representing all of the child's work. Instead, a portfolio should highlight a child's best efforts across specific domains. Since children with autism tend to develop at a pace that is quite different from their peers, the portfolio is a venue that will demonstrate and document that change. An additional benefit of the portfolio is that it allows the teacher to see and document skills as they emerge. By knowing when a skill is emerging, the teacher can plan instruction that will encourage the child to continue developing that specific skill.

Teachers with access to digital cameras can load samples of a child's work onto a CD for documentation in an electronic portfolio. This can be shared with the child's parents, with a copy given to them at the end of the school year. The following year, the electronic portfolio gives the child's new teacher an opportunity to see her work from the previous year. This eliminates the need to store a quantity of materials, and provides a convenient way for the child's family to see evidence of progress. Even the smallest gains can be a source of hope to parents.

Another method of assessment used for young children with autism is the anecdotal record. These are ongoing notes made by the teacher about a child's behavior or performance of a task. Anecdotal records are especially effective in documenting the events leading up to, or following, a particular behavior. An efficient way to keep an anecdotal record is to punch holes in the upper right hand corner of several index cards and keep them on a ring. This way, the teacher can hang the ring on a hook for easy retrieval and use. Notes written immediately following an event are traditionally more accurate than notes based on recall. In addition, anecdotal notes can serve as documentation to help plan new activities for the child.

The Learning Characteristics of Children With Autism Summarized

Tuning out the world

Now that you know how a child with autism relates to her world, it is time to set up an environment that is proactive. A proactive environment is ready for the child with autism and is prepared to help that child make the most of her preschool experience. Refer to Table 2-1 for a summary of characteristics associated with autism.

Table 2-1: Summary of the Basic Characteristics Associated With Autism

Characteristic	How the Child Might Act
Undesired Behaviors (Maladaptive)	Constant or repetitive behavior such as waving hands or hand-flapping Hitting self or others Tantrums Aggressive toward others
Lack of Functional Communication	Echolalia Stereotypic phrases Nonsense speech No speech/language
Problems With Social Interaction	Only interacts when something is needed Interacts with objects, not people Preoccupation with things, not people Totally in his/her own world
Obsessions	Rituals Routines that must be followed Only eats specific types of foods May be obsessed with objects such as spoons

Resources Used in This Chapter

Atwood, T. 1993. *Why does Chris do that?* London: National Autism Society.

Baker, B. L., & A. J. Brightman. 2003. *Steps to independence: Teaching everyday skills to children with special needs.* Baltimore, MD: Paul H. Brookes Publishing Co.

Cohen, S. 1998. *Targeting autism.* Berkley, CA: University of California Press.

Hanbury, M. 2005. *Educating pupils with autistic spectrum disorders: A practical guide.* London: Paul Chapman Publishing.

Harris, S. L., & M.J. Weiss. 1998. *Right from the start: Behavioral intervention for young children with autism.* Bethesda, MD: Woodbine House.

Janzen, J. E. 2003. *Understanding the nature of autism: A guide to the autism spectrum disorders.* San Antonio, TX: Therapy Skill Builders.

Janzen, J. E., & Therapy Skills Builders. 2000. *Autism: Facts and strategies for parents.* New York: Elsevier Science.

Murray-Slutsky, C. & B.A. Paris. 2001. *Exploring the spectrum of autism and pervasive developmental disorders: Intervention strategies.* New York: Elsevier Science.

Scott, J, C. Clark, & M.P. Brady. 1999. *Students with autism: Characteristics and instructional programming for special educators.* Belmont, CA: Wadsworth Publishing.

Sicile-Kira, C. 2004. *Autism spectrum disorders: The complete guide to understanding autism, Asperger's Syndrome, pervasive developmental disorder, and other ASDs.* New York: The Berkley Publishing Group.

Siegel, B. 2003. *Helping children with autism learn: Treatment approaches for parents and professionals.* New York: Oxford University Press.

Sigman, M. & L. Capps. 1997. *Children with autism: A developmental perspective.* Cambridge: Harvard University Press.

Strock, M. 2004. *Autism spectrum disorders* (*Pervasive Developmental Disorders*). Bethesda, MD: National Institute of Mental Health, National Institutes of Health, U.S. Department of Health and Human Services. (NIH Publication No. NIH-04-5511)

Szatmari, P. 2004. *A mind apart: Understanding children with autism and Asperger's Syndrome.* New York: The Guilford Press.

Wall, K. 2004. *Autism and early years practice: A guide for early years professionals, teachers and parents.* London: Paul Chapman Publishing.

Weatherby, A. M., & B. Prizant. 2001. *Autism spectrum disorders: A transactional developmental perspective,* Vol. 9. Baltimore, MD: Paul H. Brookes Publishing Co.

Key Terms

Aggression: Behavior that is harmful to others, such as biting, hitting, slapping, kicking, pinching, or pulling hair.

Anecdotal record: Ongoing notes made by the teacher concerning a child's behavior or performance of a task.

Augmentative forms of communication: An alternative way to communicate, such as a device that speaks for the child.

Beta-endorphin: A chemical in the brain that helps the body relax.

Casein: A protein found in food that contains wheat, rye, oats, barley, and dairy products.

Compulsive: Behaviors the child performs repeatedly that will be stopped and begun again, if a certain step is not performed exactly the same way every time.

Cue: A hint that is a word, gesture, or phrase.

Food jag: When the child will only eat certain foods. Some food jags are preferential, in that while they prefer one food to other foods, the child will eat non-preferred foods. Other food jags are more absolute, in that the child will only eat certain foods to the exclusion of all others.

Generalization: Being able to perform the same task, skill, or activity in a variety of settings or with a variety of people and/or different objects.

Gluten: A protein found in food that contains wheat, rye, oats, barley, and dairy products.

Life skills: Self-help skills, such as going to the bathroom or washing hands.

Maladaptive behavior: A behavior that is not common in most children or one that is so severe that it interferes with learning.

Obsession: A strong inclination toward something to the point of excluding everything else, such as collecting forks or watching the blades of a rotating ceiling fan.

Portfolio: A collection of the child's best work across a specific period. The portfolio is not intended to represent all the child's work; it should showcase a child's best efforts across specific domains.

Ritual: A pattern or way of doing something that is not logical, such as only walking on the floor instead of carpet or having to arrange food in a certain order before it can be eaten.

Self-injurious behavior: Something a child does to hurt herself, such as hitting or biting herself, in an effort to get out of a situation or an environment that is overwhelming.

Sensory Integration Disorder: An inability to filter or screen out sensory-related input.

Stereotypic behavior: A behavior that is carried out repeatedly and involves either movement of the child's body or movement of an object, such as repetitive hand flapping or saying the same phrase repeatedly.

Tantrum: Anger beyond what is normally seen in children, such as falling to the floor and screaming or throwing their bodies on the ground.

Urinary Peptide Test: A medical test to detect protein that is not fully broken down and digested by the body.

Planning for
Success:
Setting Up a Proactive Preschool Environment

I Know Children With Autism Learn Differently, But What Can I Do About It?

The best way to prepare to teach a child with autism is to get to know as much as possible about the child before he comes into the classroom. Encourage the child and his family to visit before the first day of school. This initial visit will give you time to get to know the child and give the child time to become familiar with your classroom. This visit should happen when other children are not present.

Plan activities around the child's strengths.

To help the child get ready for his new classroom, additional visits may be necessary. Most preschools already have a parent information form. However, you will need to find out much more about the child than is generally included on the form.

Below are some questions you should ask before the child arrives at school:

- What does she like to eat? Are there certain foods that she will not eat or that will cause her to react in a certain way?
- What particular interests does she have?
- Does she have a particular attachment to a certain object, toy, or activity?
- How does she communicate with others?
- What might cause her to become upset or frustrated?
- What do the parents think are her strengths?
- What do the parents think are her challenges?
- Who is her pediatrician?
- What other services has she been getting? Speech therapy? Occupational therapy?
- Are there any other children at home?
- What does the family do when she has an outburst at home?
- How much experience has she had with other children?

Most children will come to your class with an Individual Education Plan (IEP) or an Individual Family Service Plan (IFSP) already in place. However, those plans are designed to look at broad educational objectives and goals for the child and may have been written long before he arrives in your class. The IEP or the IFSP is a good tool to help you plan the child's curriculum. However, you also need to know as much as possible about the child and his preferences and experiences with others so that when he arrives you are prepared. If he was previously in a preschool or child care facility, schedule a visit with his teacher. Ideally, she would come with him when he visits your class for the first time. Your goal as the child's new teacher is to make his transition from the previous setting to your classroom as stress-free as possible for both you and the child.

How Do I Arrange a Preschool Environment for Success?

The environment should be as well-defined as possible. Each center or learning area should be clearly marked with a picture. It is also very important that you include a picture schedule in each area so the child can look at the schedule and get an idea of what is supposed to occur within that area. This will reduce anxiety. Remember, children with autism like to know what they are supposed to do, so a picture schedule is reassuring and helps the child adjust to her new classroom.

Children with autism also need a special place in the room where they can go. This should be located in the quietest part of the room, without distractions, and without all the sensory input they receive elsewhere. The quiet place should have indirect soft lighting, a chair or cushion that is comfortable for the child, and a few activities that the child likes. Make sure that you can always observe the child in whatever location you choose. This quiet center is also a place where the child can go to complete activities that are especially stressful for him. While a quiet center is especially essential for children with autism, it should be open to all children who need time to reflect and relax before returning to an activity.

Quiet centers should never be used as a form of punishment for a child, but should be used routinely to allow the child to be in a place where he feels safe and secure. The frequency and time that a child uses the quiet center will be different, depending on the needs of the individual child.

Remember that children with autism function best when they have:

◆ structure,
◆ a predictable routine,
◆ environments that are not distracting,
◆ verbal reminders of what will happen next, and
◆ picture schedules.

A quiet center should be a place where the child can go without distraction and relax.

Using a picture schedule to find out what happens next

How Do I Set Up Predictable Routines for a Child With Autism That Will Not Be Boring to the Other Children?

When setting up a daily routine for a child with autism, it is important to ensure that the child understands what you are asking him to do. Children with autism are less frustrated with predictable and organized routines. How the day begins will often determine how the child will behave throughout the day. If there is any variation in the schedule, even a minor change, it is important that the child knows before it happens.

When the child arrives, greet her and discuss the daily schedule. Interchangeable picture cards can be used to show each activity for the day. Make sure the child knows what each picture card represents. Children will need a schedule on a level that they understand. For some children, this may be an object schedule, or a simple first–then card. A first–then card is a series of picture pairs in which the first shows what happens first and the second shows what happens next. Remember that picture schedules can be very simple or quite complex.

Transitions are likely times for a child with autism to have an outburst. So, plan smooth transitions. Music makes an excellent transition tool. Use the same song for each transition so that the child learns that the song is a cue for something new to happen.

Sample First-Then cards

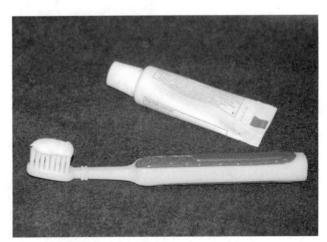

Other ideas to help facilitate smooth transitions include:

- Set a timer a few minutes before it is time to change activities; hourglass timers are less distractible than timers with bells.
- Tap the child gently on the shoulder as a cue that it is almost time to stop.
- Walk over to the picture schedule and point to the next activity.
- Ring a service bell or small chime, such as wind chimes (remember not to overwhelm with loud noises), as a reminder that it is time to change activities.
- Avoid flashing lights on and off—this is not a good method to use for signaling transition. The sensory stimulation for a child with autism will be overwhelming.

What Can I Do to Make All Children Feel Part of the Class?

In everything you do as a teacher, adopt a philosophy that values each child as a member of the class. Adopting this philosophy goes beyond using the right words or putting up pictures showing children with disabilities. It means that your actions and activities demonstrate your belief that all children can learn.

When planning for children with disabilities, keep these points in mind:

Every child is a member of the class. A member of the class has the same rights and responsibilities as his classmates and the expectations for him are matched to his abilities.

Working together helps everyone feel part of the class.

Treat others the way you want them to treat you. Model how to be a friend and how friends act toward each other.

Consistency and structure work best for children with autism. While flexibility is important, it is also important to remember that children with autism become very upset and frustrated when people are inconsistent with them and when schedules are disrupted.

Everyone can participate in some way. Even children with severe disabilities can partially participate in activities.

All children have strengths and weaknesses. Learn to identify a child's strengths and plan activities that are geared to enhance the areas where she is strong.

Nothing is free and no one is automatically entitled to anything. Communication is perhaps the most important social skill of all. Teach children how to ask for what they want and need verbally, by using signs, or with gestures.

Learned helplessness cannot be tolerated. In other words, just because a child has a disability or is challenged in some way does not mean that he cannot learn to be as independent as possible. When everything is done for a child he will learn how to be helpless and automatically expect the adults in his world to do things for him.

Water play is a fun group activity.

Children learn from each other. Arrange the environment so that children have many opportunities to practice new skills, work in groups, and depend on each other to help solve problems.

Aggression, bullying, and making fun of others are never acceptable. What may seem like simple childish teasing can soon become bullying, which can be frightening for any child, and especially children with autism, who are very literal.

Many times, misbehaviors are just misdirected attempts to communicate. When a child throws an object or has a tantrum, look at the reason behind the action. Although the behavior is not acceptable, the reason for the behavior may be explainable and is often avoidable.

Before School Starts: A Strategy for the Teacher

This strategy works best if you can use it before the first day that the new child is in your classroom.

Strategy

What to Do

1. When you learn that a child with autism will be in your class, contact the family and request that they provide you with a copy of their child's most recent medical evaluation.

2. Contact the parents to arrange a meeting. When the parents arrive, be positive and tell them you are excited about having their child (use his name) in your class. Assure them that you want to meet to plan for his success in preschool together.

3. When meeting with parents, encourage them to invite others who work with the child as well, such as grandparents, babysitters, or extended family members. Start the meeting on a positive note and tell them you are counting on them to help you. Assure them that you hope preschool will be a positive experience for their child.

4. Ask them about their child. Remember that the child will be with you for only a few hours each day, but he is with his family the majority of the time. Parents know their children best. Even if the parents have unrealistic expectations for their child, it is not up to you to make predictions as to what can and what cannot be accomplished.

5. Avoid making promises you cannot keep, such as, "I promise Tom will have a great year and make many new friends." Instead, say, "I hope Tom will have a great year. I will try to help him make friends."

6. Educate yourself about the child's disability. Find out as much as you can about the child's schedule and how he learns best. Avoid falling into the trap of trying to cure the child. Instead, look for ways to help him develop his strengths.

7. Begin the year with a commitment to yourself to always tell the parents one positive thing that their child has done before you discuss any weaknesses.

8. Remember to take notes throughout the meeting. Jot down any questions you might want to ask before the parents leave.

Objective

To help the preschool classroom teacher feel comfortable and confident when children with special needs, specifically autism, join the class

When to Use This Strategy

When you learn there will be a child or children with special needs in the classroom

Materials Needed

Notebook or folder for taking notes during the meeting

9. Set an example for others in your center or school by always using people-first language and referring to the child as a child with autism. For example, avoid describing or referring to the child as, "that autistic child" or "that emotionally disturbed child." Do not refer to the child's problems—instead, talk about the weaknesses as challenges.

Helpful Hints

◆ Don't be too hard on yourself. You will make mistakes, but you will also learn a lot in the process.

◆ Remember that working with children is stressful, and that working with children with special needs can add to that stress. Take care of yourself. Learn to take a deep breath, relax, and keep the challenges in perspective.

◆ Ask for help. Asking someone to help you with a child's behavior or with making curriculum adaptations shows that you are experienced enough to know when you need extra support.

◆ If you focus on the child's abilities, rather than his disabilities, your experience will be much more enjoyable.

Laying the Foundation: Starting From Day One

Try to anticipate the needs and preferences of the child before he arrives, keeping in mind that there will always be things you did not anticipate.

What to Do

1. Study your notes from the initial parent meeting and any other information you have received about the child.

2. Make a list of the child's preferences. Include his favorite story, songs, and activities on the list. Remove or eliminate things that may make him uncomfortable, like certain noises or smells. If you find out the name of his pet or sibling(s), write it down for future reference.

3. Go through each center and do an environmental check.

4. Ask yourself the following questions: Are there activities she might enjoy? Have I designated a quiet place for her to get away and calm down, if needed? Is each area or center clearly marked with a picture so that it is easily identifiable? Have I made a picture schedule of what will happen throughout the day and is it posted in a prominent place?

5. Review your procedure for choosing centers or activities. How do the children move from place to place? Is the method one that all children can use? For example, if each center has a necklace that children wear when they are in that center, is it something that the child with autism can easily learn to do?

6. If school is already in session, consider the children already in your class. Who might be a good peer-buddy for the child with autism? Who might be fearful of the child and need some guidance about how to treat people with disabilities? Will this be the first child in your class with disabilities? If so, do you need to talk to the class about valuing diversity?

7. Have you met with your teaching assistant and others who might come in contact with the child? Do you have a plan of action if and when things get out of control or when the child has a tantrum?

Objective

To make classroom modifications and preparations for a child with disabilities, specifically autism

When to Use This Strategy

Before the first day the child with autism is in your classroom, and if possible, before he makes his first visit to his new classroom

Materials Needed

Notes or comments written down during the initial visit with the child and his family

Laying the Foundation: Starting From Day One (continued)

8. Make a list of the child's medical issues, and any other concerns that will help the other adults (assistant teachers, volunteers, etc.) in your class feel more comfortable.

Helpful Hints

◆ Try to anticipate the needs and preferences of the child before he arrives, keeping in mind that there will always be things you did not anticipate.

◆ Remember, all parents want what is best for their child, and some parents of typically developing children in the class may have fears and concerns. Answer them honestly, assuring them that all the children in your class are valued.

◆ This may be the first time the child with autism has been in a setting with other children, and her parents may be anxious. Assure them that you will contact them, if needed. You should try to avoid letting the child's parents stay for extended periods in the class. It is important for the child with autism to learn that you are the one in charge in the classroom.

Good Morning! Good Morning!

Sometimes the child may arrive upset and need a few minutes in the quiet area before the day begins.

What to Do

1. Start each day with the same routine. It is important that you use the same words and phrases each day. You might try something like, "Good morning, (child's name)." Wait to see if the child responds. "Let's check and see what we will do first."

2. Either kneel down at eye level and show the child a picture schedule of what you want him to do, or, if you are wearing a communication apron (see page 126) point out to the child what happens first.

3. If the child does not respond to a spoken welcome, he may respond to a song. Try the following, sung to the tune of "Three Blind Mice"(first verse).

    (child's name) *welcome,*
    (child's name) *welcome,*
    I'*m glad you're here.*
    I'*m glad you're here.*

4. Direct the child to his cubby. If he hesitates, walk with him and show him. Put a picture of the child above his cubby to help him identify it more easily.

5. Tell him what to do next, "After you put away your backpack in your cubby, go to the _____ center."

6. Say or sign, "Thank you."

7. If the child does not move independently to a learning center, walk with him. Show him the picture cards that relate to putting away his backpack, coat, and so on, and then guide him to the center where he will begin his day.

Objective

To greet the child with autism and start the day on a positive note

When to Use This Strategy

When the child arrives in the morning

Materials Needed

Picture schedule of Morning Routine (see page 46)

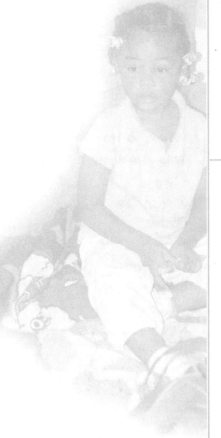

8. A child with autism likes structure and set routines. Even if you start the morning with independent center time, direct the child to a specific place each morning.

9. After he is accustomed to the routine, you can vary the welcome by giving two or more center choices. However, initially, if you tell him to choose where he wants to go, he is more likely to stand in the middle of the floor or go hide in his cubby.

Helpful Hints

◆ Keep focused on your primary objective, which is to start each day with a calm and predictable sequence.

◆ Regardless of how you start the day, consistency will make the child with autism feel more secure.

◆ Face it, some children are just not morning people and need a little more time to wake up. If the child is prone to rough mornings, then begin each day by allowing him to go to his quiet center for a few minutes, until he has adjusted to the routine.

◆ Don't forget that when you are absent, it is crucial that any substitute or teacher's assistant follow the same morning welcome routine that you follow.

"All About Me!" Bulletin Board and Book

This strategy helps the child with autism feel special and valued.

BULLETIN BOARD

What to Do

1. Ask families to send some pictures of the children and their families to school. Action pictures work best, because they show the children doing things. Ask the families to write a few sentences to go along with each picture that describe what the family is doing, and include names of the people in the pictures.

2. Feature a different child each week on the bulletin board. Put up pictures of his family and pictures of what the child enjoys.

3. After you have displayed the pictures, build an activity around them (see below). Talk about the child's siblings, pets, or activities. This helps the child feel more comfortable and helps all children in the class see the child with autism as being more like them.

BOOK

What to Do

1. Make an "All About Me!" book for each child in the class. Be sure to include pictures of grandparents, pets, activities, and customs that the family enjoys. The child can use the book throughout the year. To make the book, collect pictures of the child and the special people, pets, and places in his life. Mount the pictures on paper in the child's preferred color to enhance his use and enjoyment of the book. Invite the child to help you write a short caption or description about each picture. If the child is nonverbal or has limited communication skills, ask family members to help write the captions at home. Make sure that no more than two pictures are displayed on each page because too many pictures can be overwhelming. Place each page into a plastic sheet

Objective

To enable the child with autism to feel like a part of your class and to help his classmates get to know all about him and his family

When to Use This Strategy

When you want to help the children in your class get to know more about the child with autism

Materials Needed

Pictures and information about the child; ribbon, paper, or other materials to decorate a bulletin board and make a book

"All About Me!" Bulletin Board and Book (continued)

protector. Insert the sheets into a small notebook (a three-ring binder ½ inch wide works best). Ask the child to draw a picture for the cover or place a picture of the child's family on the cover. This will help the child identify his notebook.

2. Making a book about a child also helps connect his family to your classroom, and it can be used to help children discover things they have in common with their classmates, such as the number of brothers and sisters, types of pets, family customs, family activities, and so on.

3. An additional benefit of this activity is that, as you get to know more about the child with autism and his family, you can plan activities centered on familiar things.

Helpful Hints

◆ Be aware that not all children come from traditional families. Family is defined by the child and those he lives with, not by any traditional rule.

◆ Some children may be in foster care or come from families that are not currently intact. In this case, the All About Me activities might center on what the child likes to do and what activities he enjoys at school.

◆ It is also not uncommon for a child to be in a blended family or be in a situation where he spends some time with parents in two separate households. In this case, try to include all family members from both households.

Books That Teach a Lesson

Avoid doing this activity in groups that are so large that the child with autism is overwhelmed by the other children.

What to Do

1. Books can be important tools for helping children learn certain lessons or values.
2. Once you have identified what you want to help the child learn, such as "try, try again," conquering fears, or dealing with autism, then select a book that has that theme.
3. Whenever you read aloud, be sure to show the child that books have a title page, a beginning, and an end. Let the child hold the book while you read it to her.
4. To reinforce the concept in the book, plan activities in learning centers to support the book's lesson or value, and send a family letter home telling families that this week the children are learning to _____ and the book they are reading is _____.
5. Below are some books that teach common themes to which all children can relate.

Helpful Hints

- If the child can't attend while you read the whole book, read only part of it. When you return to read the remainder, remember to review what had happened so far in the story.
- Before reading a book about the child's disability, make sure his parents are in agreement.

Objective

To use books and stories to teach concepts that will help the child learn important lessons or skills

When to Use This Strategy

During small group instruction or when you are reading one-on-one with the child

Materials Needed

Book chosen by the teacher for a specific lesson

Book	Theme	Book	Theme
Itsy Bitsy Spider	Try, try again	*Amazing Grace*	Believe in yourself
A Chair for My Mother	Cooperation, love, and respect	*Alexander and the Terrible, Horrible, No Good, Very Bad Day*	Everyone has a bad day
Owl Babies	Fear	*Fourth Little Pig*	Fear
Going Home	Celebration	*When My Autism Gets Too Big*	Helping children with autism relax
The Three Little Pigs	Working together	*Rainbow Fish*	Learning to share
The Tenth Good Thing About Barney	Death		

This list is adapted, with permission, from *Smart Start* by Pam Schiller. Additional titles added by C. Willis.

Making New Friends

Alert the family that the child is working on introducing himself, so that they can help him practice.

Strategy

Objective

To learn how to meet new people

When to Use This Strategy

When you want to encourage the child with autism to make a new friend

Materials Needed

Cardstock or heavy paper, pencils, markers, or a picture that depicts *stop*; a picture of the child; clear contact paper or laminating machine

What to Do

1. Make a cue card with two cues. Have one for the child's name and one to remind him to wait for the other person to respond. Laminate the cue card, if possible.

2. Explain to the child that the cue cards will help him know what to do when he meets someone new.

3. Ask several children to help you and the child practice meeting people.

4. Sit in a circle and practice what to say and how to wait for the person to respond.

5. Remind the children that, when you are meeting someone for the first time, it is a good idea to look at them.

6. Look for opportunities to encourage the child to practice using the cue cards to introduce himself.

My name is Jordan.

Helpful Hints

◆ Later, when the child is familiar with this routine, add other cues, such as communicating something that he likes to do or asking the new friend to play a game.

◆ Remember to make a set of cue cards for the child to take home.

◆ Alert the family that the child is working on introducing himself, so that they can help him practice.

My New School (Getting to Know Who Works at Our School)

Wait until the child can successfully leave the classroom without getting anxious before trying this strategy.

What to Do

1. Plan ahead. Alert the other personnel in the school that you plan to bring a new child to meet them. Explain to them that the child is fearful of new people and that you are counting on them to help him feel welcome.

2. Tell the child that you are going to take him on a walking tour to meet people who work at the school.

3. Encourage him to take his introduction cue card (see previous page) with him.

4. Take the child to the people and places in the school where he might go: the library (media center), cafeteria, bus barn, custodian, school office, and so on.

5. Plan a short script for each area you visit. It will help if you use a routine that is predictable and consistent. For example, "This is the cafeteria; (worker's name) works here. She cooks the food that we eat for lunch. Introduce yourself to (worker's name)."

6. Continue until you have visited all the areas and appropriate people in the school. If you can, take a digital picture of each person and make a display in the classroom called, "People Who Work at Our School."

7. Make cards with a picture of the person's job. See if the children can match the jobs with the person who is responsible for that job.

Helpful Hints

◆ You may want to take all the children in your class to meet the people who work at the school. However, when you take the child with autism, it will be best for him if you take him alone or with one other child.

◆ Refer to the people who work at the school and their jobs, so the child will learn to associate the people at school with what they do. For example, "Miss Mary, who cooks our food." or "Mr. Thomas, who cleans our room." or "Ms. Abernathy, who is our center director."

Objective

To help the child with autism become familiar with the people he will see every day, and to help other staff members get to know him

When to Use This Strategy

After the child has been in your classroom for a few days and is getting used to the routines and the other children

Materials Needed

None

Strategy

Classroom Hunt: I Spy!

Introduce the strategy gradually—too much too soon can be overwhelming.

Objective

To encourage the child with autism to explore new areas of the classroom, interact with new toys, or try new activities

When to Use This Strategy

When you want to encourage exploration of new areas

Materials Needed

A basket with a handle, one item from each learning center

What to Do

1. Gather items that represent each of the centers in your room. For example, blocks from the block area, a magnetic letter from the literacy center, a paintbrush from the art area, a book from the reading center, and so on.

2. Place the items in a basket or box. A basket works well because you can carry it on your arm. The child may even be willing to carry it for you.

3. Tell the child that you need help putting the things in your basket back in the centers where they belong.

4. Start each hunt with the same phrase, "Here is a _____. I wonder where this goes."

5. If the child looks away or appears disinterested, try to refocus him on the item by holding it in front of him.

6. Ask, "(child's name), where do you think this goes?" (Hold up object.)

7. If he does not reply or take the object, then try to prompt him by walking to a center and saying, "Do you think it goes here?"

8. When you and the child decide the center where the object belongs, ask the child to place the item in/on the correct bin or shelf. Continue with the other objects in the basket.

Helpful Hints

◆ If the child is willing, you might try to do the activity with another child as well, so that the three of you look for the correct center.

◆ Vary the activity. If you are using picture cards, match the item to the picture card, before returning it to its proper location.

◆ Always say the name of the object.

◆ If the child acts uninterested or bored, try putting the object in the wrong place and see if he will correct you. Sometimes, even nonverbal children have an extraordinary sense of place and know in fine detail where items are usually located.

We're More Alike Than Different

This strategy helps the child with autism see that we all have strengths and weaknesses.

What to Do

1. Before beginning the activity, make a talking stick. Make one by decorating a paper towel roll, covering one end with heavy duct tape, adding uncooked rice or dried beans, and then covering the other end with duct tape. If possible, encourage each child to add something (a scrap of paper, a bit of yarn, a bit of cloth) to the talking stick until it is completely covered.

2. Place children in a small group (five or less works best). Tell them, "Today, you are going to play a game called 'This is what I like!'"

3. This game is loosely based on a Native American custom of using a talking stick, where only the person with the stick can talk.

4. Start the activity by saying, "I am first." Hold up the talking stick and say, "What I like about me is _____." Fill in the blank with something you like about yourself, such as, "What I like about me is that I enjoy singing." Pause, turn to the child on your right, and say, "What I like about you is_____" (fill in the blank with something you have observed about the child). For example, "What I like about you is that you are always kind to your friends at school."

5. Continue to pass the stick around the circle, with all of the children saying something they like about themselves, and then something they like about the person sitting next to them.

6. If the child with autism does not participate, that is okay. However, encourage the child next to him to say something she likes about him.

Helpful Hints

◆ The first time you complete this activity, place the child with autism on your right so that you can be the one to say something about him.

◆ Vary the game by adding other things like, "I am good at _____" or "You are good at _____."

◆ Encourage parents to play the game at home with their child.

Objective

To help other children become more tolerant of those who are different, especially children with disabilities

When to Use This Strategy

When you want to prepare the children in the classroom for a child with a disability, or when you want the children to learn to be more tolerant of others

Materials Needed

Empty paper towel roll, uncooked rice or dried beans, duct tape, contact paper or bits of colored paper to cover the roll, glue

Strategy

Things We Do at School (A Small-Group Activity)

The first time you play this game, place the child with autism close to you, so you can help redirect him, if necessary.

Objective

To help the child identify the various learning centers and activities he will experience throughout the day

When to Use This Strategy

When you want to familiarize children with the classroom layout and the daily routine and when you feel a child needs additional practice learning about the classroom

Materials Needed

None

What to Do

1. Before beginning the activity, tell the children that they are going to help you play a game. You will describe something in a learning center and they will tell you which center it is.

2. Place children in small groups (five or fewer works best). Begin the activity by telling them that you are going to describe a place in the room and you want them to tell you where it is. For nonverbal children, ask them to point to which center you are describing.

3. Describe a center, such as, "I am thinking about a place where we paint pictures."

4. Wait, and see if anyone raises a hand to answer the question. The child with autism may watch as other children answer. When it is his turn, use his name. For example, say, "Derek, can you tell me (or point to) the center where we play with blocks?"

5. Continue to ask questions, until everyone has had a turn.

6. Later, when everyone is familiar with the classroom, expand the game to include questions about other places at school, such as, "I am thinking about a place where we play outside." or "I am thinking about where we go when we need to go to the bathroom."

Helpful Hints

◆ The first time you play this game, place the child with autism close to you, so you can help redirect him, if necessary.

◆ Expand the activity by putting matching games into learning centers. Make a large picture card of each learning center. Then, make smaller picture cards with various items on them and ask the child to match the card to the picture of the learning center where the item would be found.

Resources Used in This Chapter

Hanbury, M. 2005. *Educating pupils with autistic spectrum disorders: A practical guide.* London: Paul Chapman Publishing.

Janzen, J. E. 2003. *Understanding the nature of autism: A guide to the autism spectrum disorders.* San Antonio, TX: Therapy Skill Builders.

Janzen, J. E., & Therapy Skills Builders. 2000. *Autism: Facts and strategies for parents.* New York: Elsevier Science.

McClannahan, L. E., & P.J. Krantz. 1998. *Activity schedules for children with autism: Teaching independent behavior.* Bethesda, MD: Woodbine House.

Schiller, P. 2002. *Start smart! Building brain power in the early years.* Beltsville, MD: Gryphon House, Inc.

Willis, C. 1998. Language development: A key to lifelong learning. *Child Care Information Exchange*, 121, 63-65.

Willis, C. 1999. Brain research implications for caregivers and teachers. *The Viewpoint.* The Virginia Association for Early Childhood Education, 2, 1-3.

Key Terms

Attend: To pay attention to or to concentrate.

Learned helplessness: When a child learns how to be helpless because he never has the opportunity to do anything for himself; instead, everything is done for him.

People-first language: Referring to the person, and then the disability.

Picture apron: An apron worn by the teacher with pictures depicting the day's schedule.

Picture schedule: A series of pictures showing what is supposed to occur within an area or time-frame.

Talking stick: A sealed, decorated tube with items inside that make interesting sounds.

Transition: Moving from one activity or area in the classroom to another.

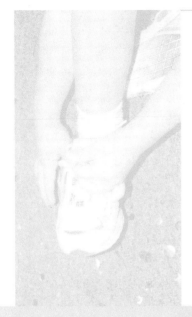

Learning
Life Skills:

What Are Life Skills?

What Are Life Skills?

Life skills have been given many names—self-help skills, everyday skills, independent living skills, and functional skills. Regardless of which term you use, these activities are the skills that children will use throughout their lives. They are skills that will help them function in daily activities and help them take care of themselves. Examples include going to the bathroom, feeding themselves, dressing themselves, brushing their teeth, taking a bath, and learning to recognize common things around them such

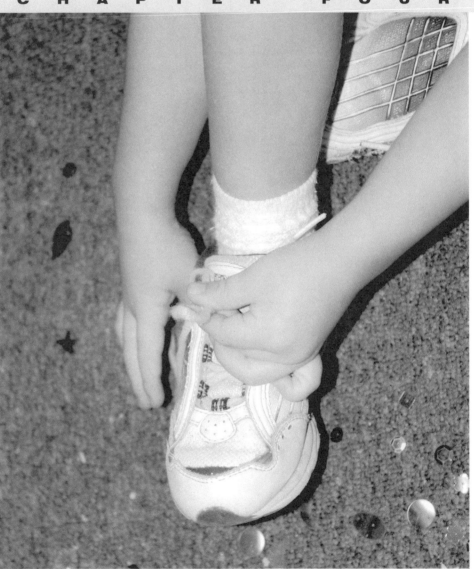

Tying shoes is an important skill.

as restrooms, exits, and stop signs. As the child gets older, these skills might include learning to access community resources, such as the bank, post office, and grocery store. For some people, life skills involve learning to ride public transportation and making simple meals at home. For preschool children, these life skills usually mean those activities that help them to become more independent.

Mastering a new skill

Why Are Life Skills Important?

Life skills are important for a variety of reasons. First, they help the child gain independence, making him feel more in control of his world. Predictability and routines are very important to children with autism, and the more they are able to take care of their own personal needs, the more predictable their daily life will be. Additionally, learning to take care of basic needs such as going to the bathroom, washing, and dressing helps the child socially. Let's face it, other children are more likely to want to interact and play with a child with good personal hygiene. Most importantly, life skills help the child's self-esteem, by giving her a sense of accomplishment and the confidence that comes from doing it "all by herself."

How Do I Teach Everyday Tasks (Life Skills)?

Work with the child's family to help determine what life skills to teach first. If the skill is a high-priority skill for the child's family, they are more likely to work with him at home to learn it. When teaching any skill, it is important that you and the child's family use the same method to teach him and practice the same skill in exactly the same way. Using the same words, phrases, and picture cues reinforces the new skill, making it easier to learn.

It is important the life skills be taught and practiced in the context of daily routines and in the environment in which that skill would likely happen. For example, you would not want to teach a child to brush his teeth while sitting at a table in your classroom. Instead, you would take him to the natural environment, in this case the bathroom, where brushing his teeth would normally happen. Likewise, you would not try to teach him the steps to feeding himself in a small-group circle. Remember that children with autism are very literal, and practicing a skill in a time or place in which that skill would not normally occur is confusing for the child, and it slows down his progress in developing that skill. Because the child is so busy trying to figure out why something is being practiced in a simulated or pretend way, he often fails to concentrate on what you are asking him to do. This chapter focuses on just those skills that will help the child with autism in his day-to-day routines at school.

Preschool life skills fall into these categories:

◆ Feeding
  ▼ Using utensils to eat
  ▼ Simple table rules
  ▼ Social context of mealtime
◆ Toileting
  ▼ Asking to go to the toilet
  ▼ Taking care of own toilet needs
  ▼ Washing hands after toileting
◆ Handling unplanned situations
◆ Self-care
  ▼ Brushing teeth
  ▼ Washing and drying face
  ▼ Tolerating a bath
◆ Dressing
  ▼ Getting dressed for school
  ▼ Getting dressed to go outside
  ▼ Taking off and putting on clothes
  ▼ Learning to select clothes appropriate for the weather
◆ Simple routines
  ▼ Getting up in the morning
  ▼ Arriving at school
  ▼ Learning the daily routine
  ▼ Getting ready to go to lunch
  ▼ Getting ready to go home
◆ Adjusting to school, after a period of being out of school (after vacation, illness, and so on)

Top: Drying hands without help
Bottom: Feeding yourself is a life skill.

What Do I Do First, Before Teaching a New Skill?

Deciding which skill to teach first involves getting input from a variety of sources and on the developmental level of the child. Begin by looking at some general guidelines to use when planning to teach any new skill.

◆ **Start by deciding which skill is the most important to the child and his family.** This decision should be based on the developmental level of the child and on the wishes of his family. It should also be based on your careful observation of the child. Trying to teach a life skill before the child is ready can be confusing, frustrating, and frightening for the child, and could result in a delay in his learning the skill.

◆ **Identify the challenges to teaching the skill you have selected**, such as the child's hyper-sensitivity to touch, her short attention span, or the child's unwillingness to tolerate water.

◆ **Inform everyone who will be working with the child** so they are aware that plans are being made to teach something new. Don't forget to include

Trying to teach a life skill before the child is ready can be confusing, frustrating, and frightening for the child, and could result in a delay in her learning the skill.

Pouring is a more advanced feeding skill.

others, such as your teaching assistant, the child's after-school caregiver, and other people with whom the child spends a significant amount of time.

♦ **Gather all the materials** you will need to teach the new skill.

♦ **Make a list of the vocabulary associated with the new skill**. Be sure to check with the child's family so that you are both using the same words and the same procedure for practicing the new skill. Children with autism do best with concrete terms; make sure you are using terms that are not confusing.

♦ **Make a task analysis or step-by-step guide for completing the skill**. Write down each step and then go over the list to see if you have left off anything important. On your list, be very detailed and describe for yourself what you want the child to do.

♦ **Make another task analysis that you will use with the child.** This list is much less detailed and simpler than the list you made for yourself. Be very specific, concise, and clear about what the child is to do.

♦ **Practice the skill several times yourself**, using the list you have made for the child. Watch yourself as you model each step. Remember, things that seem natural to you, such as hanging up a towel after you use it or flushing a toilet, may not be natural for the child.

♦ **Decide on the best time to begin implementation of the new skill**. Even if the child is not ready to do the complete task alone, she still may be ready to start learning some of the basic steps.

♦ **Make sequence cards for each step** and use simple pictures that clearly demonstrate what you are doing. Make a second set of cards to send home. It is always good to make a third set of cards as a back-up, in case something happens to the sequence cards.

♦ **Practice any new skill in the natural environment in which it would occur**. For example, the child should practice tooth brushing at a real sink in the bathroom—not at a pretend sink. The child should learn feeding skills when she is eating, and so on. Place the sequence cards in front of the child and talk about each one. Remember to use clear, concrete language.

♦ **Model each step for the child** before asking him to start the task.

toothbrush
toothpaste
lid (top for
toothpaste)*
inside
outside
rinse
teeth
mouth
top
bottom

* Lydia and Darla decide not to use the word *cap* for the top of the toothpaste, because they know that Terrance is very literal and may be confused because he uses the word cap for the hat he wears on his head.

◆ **Don't forget the home-school connection.** Keep the family involved so that what is learned at school can be reinforced at home. Generalization is often very difficult. Don't be discouraged if a skill that the child has learned at school does not immediately transfer to another environment.

◆ **Give the child time to practice one step of a skill** before going on to the next. Expecting too much, too soon, can be overwhelming for both you and the child.

How Does This All Fit Together?

Now that you have an idea about learning self-help skills, look at this example of a specific skill, such as brushing teeth. Terrance is a four-year-old in Lydia's classroom. He is not upset by water, and, in fact, Lydia has observed that he enjoys watching water as it comes out of the faucet. Lydia meets with Terrance's family, including his grandmother who takes care of him after school. Together, they determine that Terrance's learning to brush his teeth independently is a skill that is important to the family. His mother is concerned because his other brothers and sisters have had dental problems in the past, and she wants him to have healthy teeth. Lydia discusses with them the challenges that are specific to Terrance, and they remind her that he doesn't mind putting things in his mouth, but he does get upset when something is on his tongue. Lydia and her teaching assistant, Darla, find out what brand of toothpaste the family uses at home and the color and size of Terrance's toothbrush. The teachers also learn that after each meal or snack, the family takes Terrance to the bathroom and brushes his teeth for him.

After the meeting is over and the family has left, Lydia and Darla gather the materials they will need to begin teaching the new skill to Terrance. They decide they will need a toothbrush (just like the one he uses at home), toothpaste (the same brand and flavor used at home), and a plastic cup. They decide they will start teaching Terrance to brush his teeth the following day after morning snack, and make a list of the vocabulary words they will use while they are teaching him this skill (see box at left).

After reviewing the word list, the teachers decide that Terrance will need to review the concepts of *inside*, *outside*, *top*, and *bottom*, before they start teaching him the steps he needs to take to learn to brush his teeth independently. Next, they write down all the steps Terrance will need to learn to do the task successfully.

The tooth brushing task analysis includes:

1. Tell Terrance it is time to brush his teeth.
2. Walk into the bathroom with Terrance.
3. Turn on the faucet.
4. Run water over the toothbrush.
5. Pick up the toothpaste and open the lid.
6. Put a small amount of toothpaste on the toothbrush.
7. Set the toothbrush down, being careful not to let the toothpaste touch any unclean surfaces.
8. Put the lid on the toothpaste.
9. Pick up the toothbrush and lift it to his mouth.
10. Brush his front teeth.
11. Brush his back teeth.
12. Brush the teeth on top of his mouth.
13. Brush the teeth at the bottom of his mouth.
14. Spit out the toothpaste and turn on water to rinse it down the drain.
15. Put the toothbrush down.
16. Pick up the glass of water.
17. Rinse the inside of his mouth and spit out the water.
18. Clean the toothbrush and put it in a sanitary container.
19. Wipe his mouth with clean napkin or towel.

Lydia and Darla walked through each step several times and practiced modeling it for Terrance. They simplified the list by coming up with a picture schedule. The following day, they showed the picture schedule to Terrance and practiced each step together.

The hardest part for Terrance was learning to turn off the water after he had rinsed the sink. However, with practice, he learned to stop watching the water go down the drain and return his attention to finishing the sequence. After two months, he could brush his teeth independently with only minimal assistance from an adult.

Terrance became so familiar with the process of brushing his teeth that he learned to complete each step with only minimal assistance. To help him remember the parts that were most difficult, his teachers held up a picture from his picture schedule to remind him.

HOW TO TEACH A NEW SKILL

◆ Start by deciding which skill is the most important to the child and his family.

◆ Identify the challenges to teaching the skill you have selected.

◆ Inform everyone who will be working with the child that you plan to teach something new.

◆ Gather all the materials you will need to teach the new skill.

◆ Make a list of the vocabulary associated with the new skill.

◆ Make a task analysis or step-by-step guide for completing the skill. Write down each step and then go over the list to see if you forgot anything important.

◆ Make another task analysis that is much less detailed and simpler than the list you made for yourself.

◆ Practice the skill several times yourself using the list you have made for the child.

◆ Decide on the best time to begin implementation of the new skill.

◆ Make sequence cards for each step and use simple pictures that clearly demonstrate what you are doing. Make a second set of cards to send home.

◆ Practice any new skill in the natural environment in which it would occur.

◆ Keep the family involved.

◆ Don't be discouraged if a skill does not immediately transfer to another environment.

◆ Give the child time to practice one step of a skill before going on to the next.

Strategy

Communicating a Need to Go to the Bathroom

This strategy is one of three that can be used to help the child become toilet trained. This strategy is not effective after the child has already had an accident.

Objective

To teach the child to indicate the need to go to the bathroom (see page 73 for a routine for going to the bathroom)

When to Use This Strategy

When the child is mature enough and physically developed enough to handle his own toileting skills

Materials Needed

None

What to Do

1. Begin by learning the American Sign Language sign for *bathroom*. This is a very simple sign to learn. Make a fist and insert the thumb between the second and third finger. Move the hand up and down. Use this sign with all the children. It is very effective, quickly learned, and alleviates children asking aloud to go to the bathroom.

2. Once you have learned the sign, begin to use it every time the child goes to the bathroom. Make the sign and say, "_____, you need to go to the bathroom."

3. Remember that when a child is first learning a new sign, his attempt to make the sign may be similar but not exactly like the one you want him to use. This is called *approximation*. It is okay for the child to approximate a sign. However, continue to model for him how to make it correctly.

4. Meet with the child's family and encourage them to use the sign with him as well, even if the child is verbal or uses pictures to communicate. Using this sign can be very effective in his overall toilet-training routine.

Helpful Hints

◆ A sign is more effective than asking the child to use a picture card or go to a designated place and remove a bathroom permit because when children with autism need to go to the bathroom, they usually need to go immediately; waiting could cause an unwanted accident.

◆ Teach the sign to everyone who works with the child so that they can also use it with him.

Making Toileting Work

Start working on toileting skills after you have met with parents and determined that this is a priority for both the parents and the child. Do not use this strategy when the child has already had an accident or if the child consistently refuses to use the bathroom.

What to Do

1. Make a list of words that will be used: *potty, bathroom, pee-pee, poo-poo, paper, flush,* and so on. Make sure the words you use are the same words that are used at home. For example, if you say, "Do you need to go the bathroom?" and at home Mom says, "Do you need to go to the restroom?" then the child will become confused. Talk to the family and decide what words will be used for urinate and defecate. It is not a good idea to use the terms "number 1" and "number 2," as these are too abstract.

2. Brainstorm ideas and gather materials that will help the child be successful. For example, a child with tactile sensitivity will need to use very soft toilet paper. Keep in mind that once the child learns the routine, she will need practice going to the bathroom in both familiar and unfamiliar settings.

3. Make going to the bathroom a part of the regular everyday routine. Include a picture on the daily picture schedule. Later, after the child learns to associate the picture with going to the bathroom, she can learn to walk to the picture and point when she needs to go.

4. Write out each step of the process for yourself. These notes are for you. So, be specific and detailed. Make a list of what will happen first, second, and so on.

5. Make a picture schedule for going to the bathroom. Use pictures that are very specific and easily understood. Line drawings often work better than detailed color pictures.

6. Go over the picture schedule with the child before going to the bathroom. Make a game out of the activity. Talk about what happens first, what happens second, and so on.

7. Take the child to the bathroom and go through each step with her. It may be necessary for you to model for her what to do, such as pulling up her pants after she finishes or drying her hands after she washes them.

8. Encourage the child to be as independent as possible; remember that success requires consistency, patience, and practice.

9. Don't forget to praise the child for any successful attempt. Remember, the goal is for the child to learn to use the toilet independently. Communicating that she needs to go is a separate goal.

Objective

To help the child go to the bathroom independently

When to Use This Strategy

When the child is mature enough and physically developed enough to handle her own toileting skills

Materials Needed

Picture schedule for going to the bathroom

Making Toileting Work (continued)

Helpful Hints

◆ Encouraging the child to drink water or other liquid prior to practicing this routine is often helpful.

◆ Initially, practice with the child when other children are not present.

◆ Anticipate that children with autism may have additional issues with the bathroom, such as fear of sitting on the toilet, avoidance of touching toilet paper or of wiping themselves, a need to flush over and over, and a resistance to change, which may include a resistance to giving up wearing a diaper.

◆ Because children with autism don't always adapt well to new settings, anticipate that a child who is perfectly trained to use the toilet at school may hesitate to use unfamiliar bathrooms.

Bathroom Detective:
When a Child Gets Upset in the Bathroom

Use this strategy after you have begun formal toilet training and have achieved some success.

What to do

1. Try to determine the root cause of the bathroom problem. Start by looking for the obvious. Knowing that children with autism require very set routines, ask yourself the following question: What was different today? Perhaps a different person took the child to the bathroom or perhaps, rather than being the only child in the bathroom, there were several other children present.

2. Look at other factors as well. Did you insist the child go when he was involved in a favorite activity in the classroom? Did you make him go at a time that was different than when you asked him to go yesterday?

3. Immediately following the incident, take a trip to the bathroom yourself. Use the Bathroom Checklist to help you.

Bathroom Checklist

Questions	Comments
Look around the bathroom. Does it look physically the same as it did before? Even a small change such as a new color or new sign can be distracting.	
Does the child have a certain stall or urinal that he prefers? If so, was it available?	
Is the toilet paper the same as yesterday? If not, what is different about it?	
Is there an unfamiliar or new odor in the bathroom? Even the addition of a new air freshener can be upsetting for a child with autism.	
Can you see anything else that may be different than when the child previously used the restroom?	

Objective

To determine why a child resists going to the bathroom or why he gets upset when going to the bathroom

When to Use This Strategy

When the child has had some success with independent bathroom use and suddenly becomes resistant to going to the bathroom

Materials Needed

Bathroom Checklist (at left)

Bathroom Detective:
When a Child Gets Upset in the Bathroom (continued)

4. If you did not take the child to the bathroom, interview the person who did. Explain to the person that you are not criticizing or blaming him for the child's refusal to go. You just need information to help you determine what went wrong.

5. Accept the fact that you may never really know what has gone wrong, and try again later.

Helpful Hints

◆ If the child continues to be resistant, check with his parents to see if he is having a problem at home as well.

◆ The problem may be unrelated to the bathroom itself; the child may not feel well or may be constipated.

TEACHING YOUNG CHILDREN WITH AUTISM

Learning to Put on Socks/Shoes

This strategy is not effective when the child is agitated, anxious, or upset.

What to Do

1. Make a list of the steps that the child needs to follow to put on his socks and shoes. Determine if you are going to teach him to put on both socks, then both shoes, or if you are going to complete putting the sock and shoe on one foot before going to the other one.

2. Make a task analysis of each step the child will need to follow.

3. See if the child will let you model each step for him, using your own socks and shoes.

4. Ask him to watch you. Then, he should try it himself.

5. Praise him for attempting to put on his own socks and shoes.

6. Make a series of three or four picture cards to help remind him of the correct sequence in the activity. Most children have shoes that are attached with Velcro, so tying shoes is not an issue.

7. If the child appears to be sensitive about the socks or gets anxious, check and make sure they are on his foot properly. Children with autism often tend to be very sensitive when material is scratchy or does not fit properly.

Objective

To put on socks and shoes independently with minimal assistance or prompting

When to Use This Strategy

When you determine that the child has the motor skills to dress himself with minimal assistance and prompting

Materials Needed

Picture cards (3 or 4) depicting the steps to putting on socks and shoes

Helpful Hints

- Don't be overly concerned if the child refuses to take off his shoes. Many children with autism do not like to have their feet exposed to the air.
- Play games with several children where everyone takes off their shoes and socks, and then puts them back on in time to music.
- Be flexible if the child doesn't want to put on his shoes, but puts on his socks. See if he will let you help him.
- If the child continues to have difficulty, try a process called *reverse chaining*. This means you do the steps in reverse order. Instead of learning to put on his socks and shoes, you start with taking off his shoes and socks; then, reverse the process.

Strategy

Mealtime Fun!

This strategy is effective only if you have had time to discuss the child's food issues, mealtime preferences, and other meal-related issues with his family.

Objective

To make mealtime an enjoyable experience for the child and his peers

To minimize disruptions or displays of autism-related behavior during mealtime

When to Use This Strategy

After you have observed the child during a mealtime or snack time situation and are able to identify his anxieties about mealtime

Materials Needed

Poster board or construction paper in the child's favorite color, laminating materials or clear contact paper, markers for drawing on the mat

What to Do

1. Observe the child during a meal, using the Mealtime/Snack Observation Checklist on page 79. Pay close attention to other factors, such as whether he prefers to sit beside the same peer every day, whether he eats more consistently when food is presented on a plate with divided compartments, and whether he asks for more if he wants more to eat.

2. With the checklist as a guide, look at the child's preferences when planning the mealtime routine.

3. If you leave your classroom for meals, be sure to tell the child a few minutes early to allow him to get ready for meals. Go to the picture schedule posted in the classroom and point to the picture that shows eating.

4. If your class eats in a cafeteria, will other teachers take the child and walk through all the steps required to get him his lunch? It is best to practice this with the child when other children are not present. Because children with autism prefer structure and routine, it will help if the child has an assigned seat in the cafeteria.

5. For family-style eating in the classroom, model for the child how to ask for more. If the child is nonverbal, teach him the sign for "more" (see page 121).

6. Make a placemat using the child's favorite color. The mat can be made of poster board or construction paper and laminated. Draw on the placemat where each utensil will be placed—draw a large circle for the child's plate and a smaller one for his cup.

7. In the home-living area of your classroom, practice eating by having a pretend meal with the child. While he is using the placemat, demonstrate so he can practice where to put his utensils, plate, and cup.

Learning to eat with a fork is not easy.

Mealtime Fun!

8. Encourage the child to be as independent as possible at mealtime, but recognize that children with autism often experience distress over eating and may refuse to eat or refuse to try new foods.

Helpful Hints

◆ Don't try to force the child to try to new foods unless you have met with a dietitian and his family and determined that his health is at risk.

◆ If possible, reduce the light level and use indirect lighting during mealtime.

◆ Spills are a natural part of eating. If the child spills something and gets upset, talk quietly and assure him that everything is just fine.

◆ Sometimes, children with autism get so upset that they throw food or plates on the floor. When this happens, ask the child if he is finished eating and redirect him while you clean up the spill.

◆ If the child gets up and leaves the table, smile at the other children and praise them for sitting and eating with their friends. Don't try to force the child to return to the table.

◆ Make mealtime as relaxing as possible. Play soft music or talk quietly with the children while they eat.

Mealtime/Snack Observation Checklist (see below)

Observe the child periodically. Use the Mealtime Observation Checklist to help monitor the progress of the child. If the child is inconsistent in a specific area, check the block that says "sometimes." Write any comments that will help you in the box beside each question.

Ask Yourself...	Yes	No	Sometimes	Comments
Does the child sit in the same chair during meals?				
Does the child sit by the same person each time he or she eats?				
Does the child use utensils when he or she eats?				
Will the child let one food touch another?				
Does the child eat a variety of foods?				
Will the child try new foods?				
Does the child seem to have a mealtime ritual? (Folding napkin a certain way, arranging his plate a certain way, and so on)				
Does the child let you know if he or she wants more?				
Does the child let you know if he or she is finished?				

Personal Information

This is a critical survival strategy, and it is never too soon to plan for an emergency.

Objective

To teach the child to say or show personal information when asked

When to Use This Strategy

When you want to teach the child a procedure for giving personal information in an emergency situation or if he is lost and needs help

Materials Needed

Pictures of community helpers who may assist during an emergency, such as policemen, firefighters, nurses, doctors, and others

What to Do

1. This strategy works best in a small-group setting. Begin the lesson by explaining to the children that you are going to teach them a song. Tell the group that if they are lost or have an emergency they can sing this song.

2. Explain that an emergency is a situation where they can't find their parents or caregivers, or when they are lost.

3. Show pictures of firefighters, policemen, and other emergency workers (be sure to include nurses and doctors). Tell the group that if they ever need help, they should look for someone in a uniform.

4. Teach the child the following song, sung to the tune of "The Farmer in the Dell:"

My Name

My name is _____ (insert child's first name)
My name is _____ (insert child's first name)
My name is _____ (insert child's first name) *and I live on* _____ (insert name of the child's street).

5. Practice the song often and begin each time by saying, "We are going to sing this song. If you ever have an emergency and need help, you can sing the song."

6. Review the list of helpers and show the pictures again, before singing the song.

7. After the child has become familiar with the first verse, teach him the next verse:

My _____ *'s* (insert name of person child lives with such as mom, dad, or other adult) *name is* _____.
My _____ *'s* (insert name of person child lives with such as mom, dad, or other adult) *name is* _____.
My _____ *'s* (insert name of person child lives with such as mom, dad, or other adult) *name is* _____.
We live at _____ (complete address).

Personal Information

For example:

My mom's name is Sheila McDonald.
My mom's name is Sheila McDonald.
My mom's name is Sheila McDonald.
We live at 1400 West 34th Street.

Or, teach the children the following variation:
I *live with my grandmother.*
I *live with my grandmother.*
I *live with my grandmother.*
Her name is Clara Brownlow.

Helpful Hints

- ◆ Be sure to send a copy of the song home and encourage the child's family to talk about and practice the song.
- ◆ Remember that it is most likely a child will have an emergency when he is away from school so make sure all the people who know and work with the child use the song often.
- ◆ Review regularly both the song and the community helpers who can help if there is an emergency.

Strategy

All About Money

This strategy is effective only when the child is developmentally mature enough to start learning about money.

Objective

To practice money concepts

When to Use This Strategy

When the child has begun to understand number concepts

Materials Needed

Several real coins, materials for a pretend store, such as empty cereal boxes, clean coffee cans, and other items

What to Do

1. One of the most important things a child will learn is how to use money to buy the things she needs. Using money is very important to her future independence.

2. Always use real coins and talk about the relationship of one coin to another, such as five pennies in a nickel and two nickels in a dime.

3. Make a set of matching cards. To make the cards, take a picture of each type of coin (penny, nickel, dime, and quarter). Glue one picture onto each card. Encourage the child to match the coins to the pictures on the card.

4. Set up a store in your classroom where children can buy things. Let one child be the clerk and the other the customer.

5. If possible, take a community field trip to a store so that the child can purchase an item.

6. As the child becomes more familiar with how money is used, begin to use concepts, such as *more than* and *less than* when talking about money.

Helpful Hints

◆ Don't be surprised if the child picks up money concepts very quickly.

◆ Understanding the relationship between numbers and using money is a concept that comes very easily to some children with autism.

◆ If the child does not want to handle the money, allow her to use a tissue to pick it up.

Hand Washing

This strategy is not effective if the child is resistant to water and throws a violent tantrum when asked to place her hands under water.

What to Do

1. Picture sequence cards are always helpful, but this strategy depends on modeling what you want the child to do.

2. Walk with the child to the sink.

3. Tell her that you are going to play a game where you do something and then she does the same thing.

4. Say, "First, we turn on the water." Turn on the water. (Wait to see if the child turns on her faucet, too.)

5. Say, "Now, we get some soap." Put some soap on your hands. (Wait to see if the child puts soap on her hands.)

6. Say, "Next, we put our hands under the water." Put your hands under the water, and wait to see if the child does the same thing.

7. Say, "Now, we rub our hands together and count to 10." Rub soap on your hands and count to 10.

8. Say, "Next, we rinse the soap off our hands." (Wait to see if the child rinses her hands. If she does not, repeat the instructions.)

9. Say, "Finally, we dry our hands." Reach for a paper towel and dry your hands.

10. Say, "Now, we put the towel into the trash."

Objective

To establish a routine where the child independently washes her hands

When to Use This Strategy

When you have determined that the child can follow the steps for hand washing

Materials Needed

None

Helpful Hints

♦ If the child refuses to participate in the activity, help him gradually learn to accept the routine by partially participating such as doing only one or two steps before trying the whole routine independently.

♦ Remember, if the child is hesitant or resistant to any part of this routine, try to determine the cause. Maybe the towels are too rough or the water is too hot or too cold.

♦ Try to use the same words and follow the same procedure each time you practice the routine.

♦ After the child has learned the routine, see if she can do it independently.

Strategy

What to Wear?

This strategy is best to use with one or two children at a time.

Objective

To help the child begin to identify which clothes are needed for certain seasons

When to Use This Strategy

When you want to teach the child that some clothes are for cold weather and some are for warm weather

Materials Needed

Pictures of the following items: mittens or gloves, a coat, an umbrella, a raincoat, shorts, a sweater, a tank top or sleeveless light-colored shirt, 4 pictures of outdoor scenes depicting the different seasons (laminate or cover with clear contact paper) Note: If you live in a warm climate, you may wish to exclude the winter season from this activity.

What to Do

1. Show each scene and talk about it with the children. If you live in a climate that does not have cold weather, omit the winter scene. Ask the children to tell you what type of weather is shown in the picture. Ask them to explain their answers. (The child with autism may not be able to answer your questions, but he will hear the answers the other group members provide.)

2. Hold up each clothing picture. Talk about each one.

What to Wear?

3. After you talk about each picture, show the child how to attach it to the weather scene it goes with (either use tape or Velcro).

4. Ask the child to help you as you assign each piece of clothing to a specific weather scene.

5. Remove the clothing from the weather scenes and ask the children to play a game. Tell them you will hand them a piece of clothing and they can put it on the weather scene where it belongs.

6. Continue the activity until all the cards are placed on the scenes.

Helpful Hints

◆ The child with autism may resist participating. If possible, model for him exactly what he is to do.

◆ Remember to praise any attempt by the child to participate.

◆ Practice the activity often, and, as the weather changes outside, ask the child to tell you or show you what clothes he would wear in that type of weather.

◆ This is an especially important skill to learn because children with autism often want to wear the same clothes year-round and are very resistant to change, even if the weather gets colder or warmer.

Crossing the Street

This strategy is not effective when the child is absorbed in a favorite activity.

Strategy

Objective

To teach the child a song to help her remember safety rules when crossing the street

When to Use This Strategy

When you want to teach the child how to cross a street independently

Materials Needed

None

What to Do

1. Even though an adult will probably be present when a child crosses the street, it is still important that she learn what to do.

2. Try to use this strategy when you are crossing a real street; even the bus lane at your school is a street. Practice outside, so that the child learns to associate this strategy with crossing the street.

3. Teach the child the following song, sung to the tune of "Three Blind Mice."

   Stop, look, and listen,
   Stop, look, and listen,
   When you cross the street,
   When you cross the street.
   Look to the left and then to the right.
   Look to the left and then to the right.
   Remember, every time you cross the street to
   Stop, look, and listen,
   Stop, look, and listen.

4. Practice the song several times, crossing the street as you sing.

Helpful Hints

- Although children with autism don't role-play well, try singing the song and role-play crossing the street in your classroom.
- Remember to sing the song every time you cross the street with the child.
- Share the song with the child's family and other caregivers and encourage them to sing the song as they cross the street with the child, as well.

Resources Used in This Chapter

Abrams, P. & L. Henriques. 2004. *The autistic spectrum: Parent's daily helper.* Berkeley, CA: Ulysses Press.

Baker, B. L., & A.J. Brightman. 2003. *Steps to independence: Teaching everyday skills to children with special needs.* Baltimore, MD: Paul H. Brookes Publishing Co.

Cohen, S. 2002. *Targeting autism: What we know, don't know, and can do to help young children with autism and related disorders.* Berkley, CA: University of California Press.

Fouse, B. & M. Wheeler. 1997. *A treasure chest of behavioral strategies for individuals with autism.* Arlington, TX: Future Horizons.

Janzen, J. E. 2003. *Understanding the nature of autism: A guide to the autism spectrum disorders.* San Antonio, TX: Therapy Skill Builders.

Janzen, J. E., & Therapy Skills Builders. 2000. *Autism: Facts and strategies for parents.* New York: Elsevier Science.

Kluth, P. 2003. *You're going to love this kid!: Teaching students with autism in the inclusive classroom.* Baltimore, MD: Paul H. Brookes Publishing Co.

Leaf, R. (Ed.), & J. McEachin. 1999. *A work in progress: Behavior management strategies and a curriculum for intensive behavioral treatment of autism.* New York: Autism Partnership.

McClannahan, L. E., & P.J. Krantz. 1998. *Activity schedules for children with autism: Teaching independent behavior.* Bethesda, MD: Woodbine House.

Scott, J., C. Clark, & M.P. Brady. 1999. *Students with autism: Characteristics and instructional programming for special educators.* Belmont, CA: Wadsworth Publishing.

Small, M. & L. Kontente. 2003. *Everyday solutions: A practical guide for families of children with autism spectrum disorders.* Shawnee Mission, KS: Autism Asperger Publishing Company.

Sussman, F. 1999. *More than words: Helping parents promote communication and social skills in young children with autism spectrum disorder.* Toronto: The Hanen Centre.

Wheeler, Maria. 2004. *Toilet training for individuals with autism and related disorders: A comprehensive guide for parents and teachers.* Arlington, TX: Future Horizons.

Key Terms

Approximation: An inexact representation of a skill or a word that is still close enough to be useful.

Functional skills: Everyday skills that the child will use to be more independent, sometimes called self-help, life skills, or independent living skills. Functional skills are the skills a child will use throughout his life, such as brushing his teeth, going to the bathroom, and taking a bath.

Hyper-sensitivity: Overly sensitive to something, the state of being overly stimulated by the environment.

Reverse chaining: When a child starts at the end of an activity and does the process in reverse. For example, when you are trying to help a child to learn to put on his coat, in reverse chaining you would start with taking off the coat.

Task analysis: The breaking down of a skill into steps; step-by-step guide

Misbehavior or Missed Communication

Managing the Behaviors of Children With Autism

How Will I Ever Understand the Unusual Behaviors of Children With Autism?

Children with autism often have behavioral characteristics that are not typically seen in other children of the same age, such as hand-flapping or screaming out loud. Some children with autism will behave like their typically developing peers, but that behavior may be more intense or prolonged, as when a three-year-old throws a tantrum. Instead of lasting only a few

Crying can be a way to avoid something.

minutes, it lasts much longer. A challenging behavior (or problem behavior) is defined as any action where the child deliberately hurts himself, injures others, and/or causes damage to his environment. Such behaviors may socially isolate the child and further limit how others want to interact with him.

Challenging behaviors may be the result of a child who is:
◆ frustrated or confused by a new situation or activity,
◆ afraid of something,
◆ experiencing a panic or anxiety attack,
◆ extremely angry and responds by hurting herself or a classmate,
◆ very impulsive and can't seem to control his desire to do something,
◆ attached to an inanimate object,
◆ upset because a ritual has been interrupted, and/or
◆ stopped from doing something that is comforting to her.

These behaviors are very frustrating for teachers, especially when they learn that typical methods such as taking steps to help the child calm down or redirect the child's attention do not always work.

What Are Some Typical Strategies for Teachers When They Are Confronted With Challenging Behaviors?

In general, a typical response to a specific behavior is that the child acts and the teacher reacts. When a child behaves a certain way, such as hitting another child or throwing an object, the teacher must immediately determine an effective way to address the situation (react). This action-reaction cycle is often not effective in stopping the disruptive behavior of a child with autism. In fact, under some circumstances, it may make the behavior worse.

For example, some traditional teacher reactions to behavior include the following:
◆ The teacher may try to stop the child's challenging behavior by praising him when he is not doing the challenging behavior.
◆ The teacher might enforce a natural consequence for a specific action, such as when a child throws a block at another child. The natural consequence might be that he cannot play with blocks again for a given period.
◆ After the behavior has occurred, the teacher may try to talk to the child and explain why that specific behavior is not acceptable.
◆ An attempt may be made to redirect the child away from what is upsetting her, in an effort to refocus her attention on something new or novel.

The reason a traditional action-reaction cycle is not effective for children with autism is that the strategies focus on the behavior itself and not the reason behind the behavior. When working with children with autism, it is important to look at both the form (what the child is doing) and the function (why the child is doing it).

What Is Meant by Form and Function?

The form is the way the child behaves. For example, if Kara throws a book, the form of the behavior is throwing. When Michael hits himself repeatedly, the form of the behavior is self-injurious or hitting. The form of the behavior tells us what the child is doing; it does not tell us why he is doing it.

Why a child behaves a certain way can be more important than how she behaves. Understanding why helps teachers plan strategies that can often prevent the behavior from happening. The motivation (why) behind something the child does is called the function of the behavior. It is the reason or the purpose that the behavior serves. For example, Kara may be throwing the book because she is frustrated and overwhelmed by all the noise in the room. Michael may be hitting himself because the teacher tells him it is time to stop an activity that he enjoys.

There are two basic functions or reasons behind challenging behaviors. The child wants to either avoid or escape from someone or something, or wants access to something. In other words, he wants an object or an outcome and he does not have the communication skills to ask for it.

How Can I Determine the Function or Reason for a Child's Behavior?

The best way to understand why a child behaves a certain way is to examine what is going on just before or just after the behavior. This process is called a functional assessment and determines the relationship between events in a child's environment and the occurrence of challenging behaviors. This process involves:

- identifying and defining the challenging behavior.
- identifying the events and circumstances that are happening or not happening when the child is behaving in a certain way.
- determining the social reason behind the challenging behavior.

For example, Marissa goes outside and stands watching while two children throw a ball back and forth. They put down the ball and go to the swings.

Why a child behaves a certain way can be more important than how she behaves. Understanding why helps teachers plan strategies that can often prevent the behavior from happening.

Marissa starts to scream and hit herself. Watching the children throw the ball was enjoyable for Marissa. When they stopped, she was angry because she wanted to continue watching them throw the ball. In this example, the screaming was the form (type of behavior) and the children stopping was the function (reason behind the behavior). The event that she enjoyed (watching the children play ball) was taken away from her, so she responded as a way of protesting.

The events that relate to a behavior can often help determine why the behavior occurs. These are sometimes called *setting events*—conditions that occur at the same time a challenging behavior occurs. These setting events often increase the likelihood that a challenging behavior may occur. Knowing what events or conditions may cause a child to behave in a certain way helps reduce or stop a challenging behavior before it starts. The best intervention is prevention!

The following are examples of some setting events:
- staff changes or a preferred teacher's absence
- changes in medication
- sleep (too much or too little)
- sickness (even though children with autism may not express symptoms of feeling unwell in the same way as other children)
- situations that are new or demanding to the child
- environment that is chaotic and unorganized
- disruptions in the regular routine of the day, such as a fire drill or a field trip
- changes in temperature (room temperature and weather)
- waiting a long time for something she wants
- waiting too long to eat or sleep
- a preferred toy or item placed somewhere different in the classroom

While you may never be able to completely stop a child with autism from behaving in a certain way, you may be able to

Waiting for a turn is not easy.

greatly reduce his challenging behaviors by creating an environment that is proactive (preventative) rather than one that is reactive (only responds after the child misbehaves).

When planning for a positive environment, look at the following:

The type of classroom where the child is placed—Look at appropriate classroom options for the child. Sometimes, an environment or situation can be too stressful for her. The child may need less time in a regular classroom and more time in a special education class. There may be too many children in the setting or the activity level may be too intense. The school day may be too long for the child or she may need to come to school later in the day or leave earlier in the afternoon.

Curriculum—Developmentally appropriate practice in early childhood involves learning how to interact and get along with others. Interaction with others involves using social skills. Her peers will not easily accept a child with poor social skills. When peers socially reject a child, it reduces the natural opportunities for a child to learn social skills with peers and may worsen her behavior problems.

Select materials that encourage interaction.

Materials—Materials can make it easier for a child to respond in a more positive manner. Select materials that encourage interaction (for example, blocks, a ball, or a swing) and lessen the possibility of the child's reacting in a negative manner. Make sure there are enough materials and that the child does not have to wait too long for his turn.

Keep rules simple—Avoid too many rules or rules that are vague and abstract. Post them where all of the children can see them and refer to them often. Picture representations of the rules will probably help all children, including children with autism, learn and keep the rules in mind.

Make consequences natural and be consistent!—Children with autism become confused when there are inconsistencies in how and when things happen.

The keys to a child with autism being successful in a preschool setting include:

◆ a physical environment that promotes interaction and that is neither too stimulating nor too overwhelming for the child,

◆ rules that guide behavior and are simple and concrete,

◆ materials that encourage persistence and attention,

◆ routines that are easily followed and understood, and

◆ transitions that are simple and clear.

COMPONENTS OF A FUNCTIONAL ASSESSMENT

- Identify and define the challenging behavior.
- Identify the events and circumstances that are happening or not happening when the child is behaving in a certain way.
- Determine the social reason behind the challenging behavior.

How Do I Know What Procedure to Use?

What strategy you use depends on several factors. First, you must select a behavior that both you and the child's family wish to change. Second, you must decide if the function of the challenging behavior (either to escape/avoid or gain access) is acceptable. For example, if Meleka throws a tantrum every time you ask her to stop working in the manipulative area and come to circle time, you might decide that you can honor her reason (not wanting to stop) and teach her how to let you know

A communicative replacement—"more."

that she wants more time before coming to the circle. When a child learns to replace a negative behavior with a more acceptable behavior, such as letting you know she needs more time, you are teaching her to use a communicative replacement.

A *communicative replacement* is a form of communication or a message that the child gives you to replace the behavior. Let's look at an example of using a communicative replacement in this situation. You may help Meleka know when it is time to make a transition by giving her an unbreakable hourglass and telling her that when the sand runs out, it will be time to leave the manipulative area and come to the large group circle. She will have more control observing the hourglass and knowing that there will be a given time to go to the circle, which may lessen her stress about it.

There may be some functions you cannot honor. For example, if Micah screams and hits himself every time you ask him to eat something, then you might decide that the function or reason for his behavior is to escape eating his lunch. You cannot honor this because you know that he has to eat lunch at school. In this instance, use a strategy that would help Micah control his behavior, but not allow him to escape eating. For example, let him listen to his favorite music while he eats or allow him to make choices about what he eats. He might prefer to eat alone with headphones on; while this does little to encourage socialization, it does disrupt the cycle of hitting himself at lunch time. In other words, the procedure or strategy you select depends on if you can honor or allow the reason behind the child's behavior.

Rejecting an Optional Activity

The child uses this strategy once he is engaged in an activity and wants to escape or stop the activity, and when the teacher has indicated ahead of time that she can stop the activity as long as he uses an appropriate rejecting response. Remember, there are some activities that are not optional, such as taking medication.

What to Do

1. Before the activity begins, the teacher says that the activity will be a free-choice activity and the child may reject or stop participating in the activity whenever he chooses as long as he does so in a predetermined way.

2. The teacher removes a small service bell from a container with a lid (whipped topping containers work well), and puts the lid back on the container. The teacher then places the empty container back on the shelf and explains to the child that when he wants to stop, he can ring the bell.

3. The service bell is placed near where the child is working. The teacher rings it one time. This serves as a cue to the child that this particular activity is one that he can choose to stop.

4. When the child wants to stop the activity, he rings the service bell. The teacher comes and says, "Oh, you want to stop now."

5. The teacher offers the child another activity and directs him to the activity. The teacher picks up the service bell and places it back into the container and removes the container from the area.

6. It is important that the child learn that not all activities can be stopped. That is why the bell should only be visible to the child when he is involved in an optional activity.

Objective

To teach the child to use appropriate behavior and communicate that he rejects or wishes to stop an activity

When to Use This Strategy

When the teacher has identified the option for a child to reject or stop an activity

Materials Needed

Small service bell or hand-bell

Helpful Hints

◆ Once a history of escape has become associated with an event, a child may begin to anticipate the onset of the activity and attempt to avoid it.

◆ Initially, designate only one or two activities a day that the child can choose to stop and not return to finish.

◆ This strategy is not the same as the strategy the child might use to let you know he just needs a break. In this strategy, the child does not have to return to the original activity.

Space Invaders!

This is a proactive strategy and will not be effective after the child is already upset.

Objective

To help the child learn to signal when someone is too close to him and he feels threatened by their nearness

When to Use This Strategy

When a peer approaches a child with autism and you can tell by the child's posture or behavior that the peer is standing too close

Materials Needed

Tongue depressor, glue, picture of a silly looking space alien (if possible, encourage the child to color the picture)

What to Do

1. Work with the child to make a picture of a space alien. Glue or tape the space alien picture onto a tongue depressor, making a stick puppet. An alternative to this would be a hand puppet made from a sock.
2. Explain that whenever another child gets too close, the child with autism can either raise his stick puppet or put the hand puppet on his hand.
3. Ask for a peer volunteer and model how to use the hand puppet so that all the children in the room understand that when the child with autism raises his puppet he is trying to say, "You are standing too close to me!"
4. Explain that the child is saying that he wants the invader to step back before trying to talk or play with him.
5. Ask for some volunteers and practice the activity together.
6. Place the puppet in a location where the child with autism has easy access to it.
7. Remember to reward the child verbally when he attempts to use this strategy instead of behaving in an inappropriate manner.

Helpful Hints

- Sometimes children with autism need extra practice before they can use a strategy consistently across situations.
- Play a game with this strategy so all the children in the class know how and why the child uses his puppet.

Asking for a Work Break

The important thing to remember with this strategy is that it is crucial that the child returns to the activity after the break.

What to Do

1. Cut cardboard or heavy card stock into two squares approximately 8" x 8".

2. Make a two-sided sign. Write or paint "Stop" in red on one side and "Go" in green on the other side. A picture card meaning "stop" and one meaning "go" can also be used. Mount one of the signs on each side of a block of wood.

3. Play a game where the child turns the sign to red for "stop" and green for "go." Practice the game several times.

4. Explain the three rules to this game:

    ◆ The child can only use this strategy when the teacher gives him the stop/go sign.

    ◆ The child can take a break but must return to the activity when the break time is over.

    ◆ If the child does not honor the rules, he may lose his chance to request a break.

5. Initially, honor the child's request to take a break every time he asks to do so by turning the sign from green to red. Later, if he is using the sign too much and taking multiple breaks, you may choose not to honor his request.

6. Have a pre-specified break place where the child can go. This may be a quiet area in your room or a place where the lights are lowered. Explain to the child that, when you tell him his break is over, he must return to the activity.

7. Direct the child to take the sign into the break area with him. When it is time to return to the activity, walk into his break area and turn the sign from red to green. This designates that it is time to return to the original activity.

8. If the child does not return, or begins to throw a tantrum, remove the sign and gently guide him back to the activity. If he continues to resist, sit with him. It is critical that he returns to the activity, once he has taken a break.

Helpful Hints

◆ Remember that, if the child uses this strategy consistently and returns to work after his break, then he will have more opportunities to take breaks.

◆ This strategy is different from the rejecting strategy, because this one is used when the child needs to stop and return to something.

◆ An alternative is to make a cloth flag and mount it on a small pole made from a dowel rod. The child raises the flag when he wants a break and lowers it when he returns from the break.

Objective

To teach the child to request a break or a time away from an activity, so he can relax

When to Use This Strategy

When the child is becoming overwhelmed by the environment or getting frustrated with an activity or situation

Materials Needed

Cardboard or heavy card stock, colored markers or pencils, a small block of wood

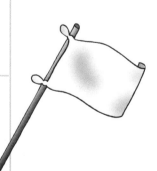

Distract and Redirect

This strategy is most effective when the distraction is a preferred item or activity, and when the child is not upset, overly tired, or anxious.

Strategy

Objective

To distract or redirect a child from one activity to another

When to Use This Strategy

When you feel that the child is becoming upset or spending too much time fixating on a particular object or activity

Materials Needed

A preferred item or a pre-selected activity

Redirect to a favorite activity

What to Do

1. Walk up to the child and start to hum his favorite song ("Wheels on the Bus," "Itsy Bitsy Spider," or "Where Is Thumbkin?"). This will get his attention in a way that does not alarm him or upset him.
2. Point to the place or item that you wish to redirect the child toward.
3. Look at the child, then look at the item.
4. Gently guide him toward the new object or activity. If he does not follow you, gently reach out and take his elbow or hand.
5. Walk slowly together toward the object.
6. Sit down with the child and hand him the object.
7. Smile at him and stay a few minutes while he explores the new object.

Helpful Hints

◆ Children with autism often do not like to be redirected from an activity or object that they are involved with. Try standing beside the child and humming for a few minutes before you start redirecting him to the new activity.

Waiting

This strategy can be used when the child is waiting in line for something, such as in the cafeteria or at the water fountain. It works best with small groups of children. Larger groups can be overwhelming and the child will have to wait too long for a turn.

What to Do

1. Give the child something to do with her hands while she waits. A squishy toy or a soft squeezable object works best.
2. Play music that is soft and enjoyable so all the children have something to listen to when they are waiting for a turn.
3. If the activity is one that can be counted, such as each child gets two tries to throw a beanbag into a box, ask the child with autism to help you count as each child takes a turn.
4. When you are beginning to teach this strategy, let the child go second or third. Waiting too long the first few times can cause her to be too anxious.
5. Later, when the child has learned to wait, place her further back in the line.
6. Verbally praise the child for waiting her turn.

Objective

To help the child learn to distract herself while waiting for her turn

When to Use This Strategy

When members of the class or a small group of children are involved in an activity in which the child has to wait for her turn to do something

Materials Needed

A preferred item or a pre-selected activity

Helpful Hints

◆ If you play music, teach the child a few body movements that she can do while waiting.
◆ As each child steps forward to take a turn, verbally announce who will be next. For example, "After Derrick finishes it will be Althea's turn."
◆ Try using first-then cards, which show what a child must do *first*, before *then* getting to do a preferred activity.

Strategy

Change in Routine

When first using this strategy, introduce changes that might produce low or controllable levels of the child's challenging behavior (brief and/or low to moderate intensity whining and crying), rather than severe screaming and aggression.

Objective

To help the child accept a change in the daily routine without becoming upset or displaying disruptive behavior

When to Use This Strategy

When you know there will be a change in the daily routine, such as a speaker, special program, fire drill, or other interruption

Materials Needed

Child's daily schedule cards and additional cards to depict the change

What to Do

1. Begin by making some planned changes in a child's schedule, to give him (and you) opportunities to learn how to deal with such changes.
2. Walk with the child to where his daily schedule or schedule cards are displayed. It is a good idea to attach the cards to the display board or wall with Velcro so that you can change them easily.
3. Talk about the schedule and what will happen next. Show him the new card that you have made and describe what the card represents. For example, "Today we are having a special music concert after center time. I made a picture for you." Show the picture to the child.

4. Remove the card that the new picture will replace and attach the picture to the schedule.
5. Talk about the change in schedule. Right before it is time for the concert, show the card that represents the concert to the child.
6. Remind the child that this is a special activity and tell him that tomorrow the schedule will return to what he is accustomed to.
7. In order for the child to discriminate occasional activities from regular routine activities, try making the special activity card on a different colored background such as yellow or pale orange. Be consistent. Every time there is a new occasional activity, depict it on the same color. In time, the child will come to identify that all activities pictured on that color card will be special or occasional in nature.

Helpful Hints

♦ Once the child responds appropriately, with the assistance of the schedule cards in these situations, then you can introduce changes in routine that are likely to result in more severe behaviors.

Hands at Home

This strategy is particularly effective when you are moving the child from one setting to another. It is least effective when the child has already become so stressed she is tensing her body and preparing for an outburst.

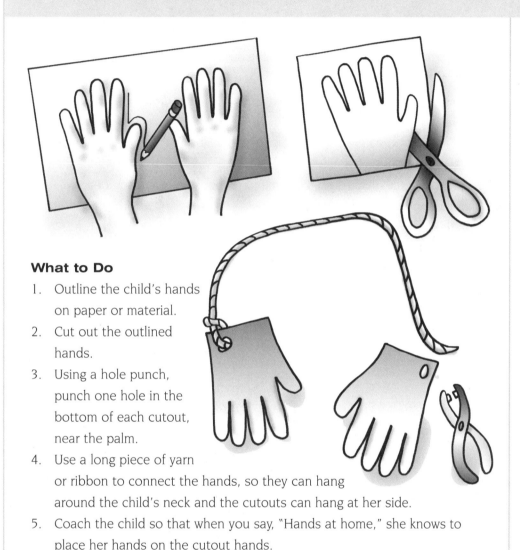

What to Do

1. Outline the child's hands on paper or material.
2. Cut out the outlined hands.
3. Using a hole punch, punch one hole in the bottom of each cutout, near the palm.
4. Use a long piece of yarn or ribbon to connect the hands, so they can hang around the child's neck and the cutouts can hang at her side.
5. Coach the child so that when you say, "Hands at home," she knows to place her hands on the cutout hands.
6. After the child learns the activity, you can change to just raising your hand slightly, such as when you wave at someone, to cue her to put her hands on the cutout hands.

Objective

To help the child keep her hands at her sides, therefore reducing stereotypical behaviors such as hand flapping and hand wringing

When to Use This Strategy

When you want the child to attend to what you are saying and during times of transition

Materials Needed

Paper, scissors, glue, laminating machine, string or yarn, hole punch

Helpful Hints

◆ Remember that many children with autism have difficulty touching certain textures and materials. Be sure to use paper that is of a color and texture that the child can tolerate.

Strategy

Environmental Hazard

This strategy should be used to teach the child to inform the teacher that she needs to modify the environment so that the child can remain in that environment. It is not to be used to help the child take a break.

Objective

To provide a method for the child to let the teacher know as soon as the environmental stimulation is becoming overwhelming

When to Use This Strategy

When the child needs a very quick and effective method to tell the teacher that something in the environment needs to be toned down

Materials Needed

None

What to Do

1. In a small group setting, introduce the strategy as a game. Explain that you are going to make a noise. If it is too loud, the children are to cover their ears.

2. Make a noise and demonstrate that it is too loud by placing your hands over your own ears. Repeat the activity, indicating when something is too bright by closing your eyes.

3. Encourage the child to do the same sign or gesture when something is either too loud or too bright for him.

4. In time, the child learns to cover his ears or his eyes as a cue to the teacher that something needs to be changed.

Helpful Hints

◆ This strategy can be used with other senses as well.

Today, I Feel...

This strategy should be enjoyable for the child so that she learns to express how she is feeling.

What to Do

1. Make a set of feeling cards. Begin with two: *happy* and *sad*. Later, you might add other cards such as *mad*, *surprised*, and so on.

2. Talk about each card. Identify the emotion for the child. Hold up the card with the happy picture and say, "This card shows a feeling. This is happy."

3. Show the child the card that describes what you say. For example, say, "It makes me happy when I see children play." Then, hold up or point to the card showing happy.

4. Repeat the same activity using sad. Say, "It makes me sad when _____." Hold up or point to the card showing sad.

5. Ask the child a question to see if she can point to the card that best describes how she feels. For example, "How does it make you feel when you fall down?" Then, after waiting for a response, point to the picture of sad.

6. Throughout the day, use the cards and ask the child a question. If she points to the card, verbally respond with, "Thank you for telling me how you feel."

7. Use the cards until the child understands that the cards describe an emotion. It may take several days or weeks. Mount the cards near the child's picture schedule and encourage her to point to them to tell you how she is feeling.

Helpful Hints

◆ Mount the cards in several places, so the child will have access to them.

◆ Add other cards to the feelings picture cards.

◆ After the child is familiar with the activity, use them when she is just starting to get upset about something—before she begins to behave inappropriately.

Objective

To help the child learn to communicate her emotional state

When to Use This Strategy

When you want to know how a child is feeling or when you want to help the child learn to self- monitor her feelings

Materials Needed

Picture cards depicting *happy*, *sad*, and *mad*

STRATEGIES TO HELP MANAGE BEHAVIOR

Help Me Solve a Problem

The child with autism may not initially want to participate. Try to encourage him to help the group decide what to do.

Objective

To help the child answer questions involving behavior

When to Use This Strategy

When you are working with a small group of children

Materials Needed

A large sack or gift bag, sentence strips

What to Do

1. Before the children join the circle, describe typical classroom situations by writing a series of statements on the sentence strips and putting them in a bag. For example: Two children want to use the sink at the same time. You want to go to the library center and it is full. Someone hit you. There is too much noise in the room and it hurts your ears. No one will play with you.

2. When the children come to the circle, tell them you are going to play a game with them. Reach into the bag and pull out a sentence strip.

3. Read the sentence aloud, and ask, "What should I do?" Wait, to see if anyone wants to answer the question.

4. Let each child draw a sentence strip from the bag. Help them read the sentences, and talk in the group about what can be done to solve the problem.

5. Repeat the process until everyone has taken a turn.

6. Tell the group that you will play the game again soon.

Helpful Hint

◆ Share with parents what you are doing, and see if they have any suggestions for things you can write on the sentence strips the next time you play the game.

TEACHING YOUNG CHILDREN WITH AUTISM

Resources Used in This Chapter

Abrams, P. & L. Henriques. 2004. *The autistic spectrum: Parent's daily helper.* Berkeley, CA: Ulysses Press.

Baker, B. L., & A.J. Brightman. 2003. *Steps to independence: Teaching everyday skills to children with special needs.* Baltimore, MD: Paul H. Brookes Publishing Co.

Baker, Jed E. 2003. *Social skills training: For children and adolescents with Asperger syndrome and social-communication problems.* Shawnee Mission, KS: Autism Asperger Publishing Company.

Cohen, S. 2002. *Targeting autism: What we know, don't know, and can do to help young children with autism and related disorders.* Berkley, CA: University of California Press.

Fouse, B. & M. Wheeler. 1997. *A treasure chest of behavioral strategies for individuals with autism.* Arlington, TX: Future Horizons.

Gutstein, S. E. & R. Sheely. 2002. *Relationship development intervention with young children: Social and emotional development activities for Asperger syndrome, autism, PDD and NLD.* London: Jessica Kingsley Publishers.

Hanbury, M. 2005. *Educating pupils with autistic spectrum disorders: A practical guide.* London: Paul Chapman Publishing.

Harris, S. L., & M. J. Weiss. 1998. *Right from the start: Behavioral Intervention for young children with autism.* Bethesda, MD: Woodbine House.

Kluth, P. 2003. *You're going to love this kid!: Teaching students with autism in the inclusive classroom.* Baltimore, MD: Paul H. Brookes Publishing Co.

Leaf, Ron (Ed.), & J. McEachin. 1999. *A work in progress: Behavior management strategies and a curriculum for intensive behavioral treatment of autism.* New York: Autism Partnership.

MacDonald, L. 2000. *Learning interrupted: Maladaptive behavior in the classroom.* Retrieved from http://www.mugsy.org

McClannahan, L. E., & P.J. Krantz. 1998. *Activity schedules for children with autism: Teaching independent behavior.* Bethesda, MD: Woodbine House.

Siegel, B. 2003. *Helping children with autism learn: Treatment approaches for parents and professionals.* New York: Oxford University Press.

Williams, D. 1996. *Autism: An inside-out approach: An innovative look at the mechanics of autism and its developmental cousins.* London: Jessica Kingsley Publishers.

Key Terms

Challenging behavior: A problem behavior defined as any action where the child deliberately hurts himself, injures others, and/or causes damage to his environment.

Communicative replacement: A form of communication or a message that the child gives to you that replaces the behavior.

Form: The way a child behaves. Examples of forms of behavior are hitting, biting, and so on.

Function: The reason why something happens. The function of a behavior is the reason behind the behavior.

Functional assessment: An evaluation designed to determine the relationship between events in a child's environment and the occurrence of challenging behaviors.

Natural consequence: The logical result of an action.

Proactive: A procedure or action that happens before a problem occurs and is designed to prevent the problem or behavior from occurring.

Setting event: Conditions that occur at the same time a challenging behavior occurs.

Signs, Symbols, and Language:
Helping a Child Communicate

What Exactly Is Communication?

For the purposes of this book, we will define communication as an interaction between two or more people where information is exchanged. In other words, when one person sends a message to another person, we say they are communicating. Three aspects of communication (see Table 6-1 on the next page) determine how well a child learns to communicate: form, function, and content.

Using communication in a social setting

Table 6-1: Aspects of Communication

Communication	Definition	Example
Form	A way to communicate	Crying, talking, gestures, sign language, pointing to picture cards
Function	A reason to communicate	Hungry, want something, need something or someone, need attention
Content	Purpose of communication	The child needs experiences and opportunities to explore, so that he will have something to communicate about

How Do Children With Autism Communicate Differently Than Typically Developing Preschool Children?

Language disorders are often widely accepted as typical of children with autism. In fact, it may be the most noticed characteristic. A language disorder is defined as a deficit in using words or vocabulary. It can also involve how a child understands language and uses it in social settings. For children with autism, a pragmatic language delay is often seen. Pragmatic language involves using language in a social setting. For example, knowing what is appropriate to say, when to say it, and the general give-and-take nature of a friendly conversation. Because autism is a spectrum ranging from severe to very mild, children with autism will have communication abilities that range from not talking at all (nonverbal) to being able to communicate very well. Often, children with autism who talk will appear to use words and speech in a way that is not meaningful or non-functional.

What Do You Mean by Communication That Is Not Meaningful?

Non-functional communication is speech that is understood and spoken clearly but has no relevance to the interaction that is taking place. For example, four-year-old Evan knows how to talk and does so frequently, but when you ask him to go outside, he simply says, "Bottom of the ninth and the bases are loaded." Evan is communicating. In fact, he is answering her question. Unfortunately, he is answering it in a non-functional manner. However, sometimes what sounds like non-functional communication can, with careful observation, be the child's way of answering in a way that makes sense to him. In other words, there are times when non-functional communication from a teacher's perspective is functional for the child. What Evan really means is, "Going outside is very stressful."

How Can Non-Functional Communication Be Functional for the Child?

To answer this question, let's examine how Larry answers questions. He is five, knows about colors, and can name and describe each of them. However, when asked, "Larry, what is your favorite color?" he replies, "Lemon yellow." On the other hand, when asked, "Would you like to go to the block center?" he replies "Crimson red." It appears that he is answering the first question appropriately or functionally, while his answer to the second question is non-functional and not appropriate.

Larry's teacher has been observing his communication for some time and has determined that every time Larry responds with "crimson red" it is Larry's way of saying "No!" He has also observed that when Larry means "yes," he answers with "sunset orange." His teacher, through observation and experience, has learned to interpret the meaning behind Larry's non-functional communication. But it does not mean that Larry's teacher needs to stop encouraging him to answer "yes" or "no." It means that, while he is learning to answer "yes" and "no," his teacher, at least, knows how to interpret the way in which Larry is currently expressing his wishes.

Children with autism who have difficulties with functional communication may use echolalia when responding to teachers and caregivers. It can be very frustrating as a teacher when everything you say is repeated back to you.

There are times when a child with echolalia is not even aware he is doing anything out of the ordinary.

What Exactly Is Echolalia?

Echolalia is the echoing and repetition of a phrase or word. This is especially common in some children with autism who do not use speech functionally. Echolalia can be an instant response—meaning that the child will repeat a phrase immediately after it is heard. For example, the teacher says, "Time for small group" and the child immediately repeats, "Time for small group." A child might repeat the phrase multiple times, "Time for small group, time for small group, time for small group." Often, echolalia cannot be controlled or stopped on command. There are times when a child with echolalia is not even aware he is doing anything out of the ordinary.

Sometimes, children use echolalia as a way to intentionally communicate. The repeated phrase has meaning to the child, and they attempt to use the phrase in conversation. For example, when mom asks Bailey about her day at school, Bailey might respond with the phrase "time for small group," as a way to communicate that she went to group at school.

Delayed echolalia occurs hours, days, or weeks after it is first heard. This type of echolalia is unpredictable and may happen because a child hears a phrase he likes. For example, Dusty heard the expression, "Beam me up, Scotty!" from the television series *Star Trek*. He used the expression over and over all day long, much to the frustration of his teacher. However, when the teacher observed the context or the situations in which he used it most often, she found it was when he was frustrated or when a new activity had been introduced. In his own way, Dusty was using the phrase, "Beam me up, Scotty!" to express his anxiety over the new task. While the expression in itself made no sense to others, for Dusty, it had meaning.

Paula Kluth, in her book *You're Going to Love this Kid*, makes several suggestions as to how a person might respond to echolalia. First, she suggests that the listener reassure the child. A teacher might say, "I think you are trying to tell me _____." or "I am sorry. I don't understand. Are you trying to tell me _____?" The response of the teacher is an attempt to show the child that she is listening and encourages the child to keep trying to let her know what he wants.

Her second strategy is called going to the movies, which means that when a child repeats a phrase from a movie or television show, the teacher tries to determine if the child is using that phrase to communicate a message. Once the teacher has figured out what the phrase means to the child, she can make a key for others to follow. For example, Dusty uses the phrase, "Beam me up, Scotty!" when he is frightened because to him, it means, "I'm scared and don't understand what to do next."

Another technique for handling echolalia is to use it to your benefit. For example, you ask the child, "Do you want a cookie?" and the child replies, "Do you want a cookie?" You then say what you want the child to say, "Yes, I want a cookie." This allows you to build the relationship between what the child says and what is intended.

Finally, the work of Gail Gillingham has suggested that some children with echolalia respond better when the person who is talking with them whispers. The idea is that the listener becomes occupied with trying to hear the speaker and doesn't respond with echolalia.

Why Do Children With Autism Have So Much Trouble Communicating?

Effective communication is more than just sending and receiving messages. It requires that one person, either the sender or the receiver of the message, interact with the other person. Actually, for the interaction to be successful, the other person must reciprocate in some way. In initiating an exchange of a message or information, the sender must be willing to approach the person she will be communicating with. Although the child with autism may be able to answer a direct question or make a statement about what she wants, starting a conversation is especially difficult. In fact, a child with autism will more likely initiate a communication when she wants or needs something. It is less likely she will initiate communication simply for the sake of a social interaction.

It is generally agreed that communication can be divided into expressive and receptive. Expressive communication has to do with how the child inputs his message to the person receiving it. In other words, how he uses communication to express himself. Receptive communication is how the child receives messages or information from others. Speech-language pathologists and other experts in the field of communication have always believed that a child can receive messages much earlier than he can generate them. Therefore, a child's receptive language develops before his expressive language.

Speech-language pathologists are excellent resources for helping determine not only how and why a child communicates, but what can be done to enhance his communication. For a child to communicate effectively, he must be able to communicate on purpose. This is called intentional communication.

Although the child with autism may be able to answer a direct question or make a statement about what she wants, starting a conversation is especially difficult.

What Is Intentional Communication?

Asking a friend to play by using a picture

Intentional communication is communication that happens for a reason. It is purposeful. For example, when babies are first beginning to experiment with sound, they may repeat the same sounds over and over again. For example, a baby may say "ba-ba-boo-boo-ba-ba-boo-boo" repeatedly. This experiment with sound is probably pre-intentional communication; she is most likely experimenting with sound and enjoys the way it feels to say it over and over.

However, if when she says, "ba-ba-boo-boo-ba-ba-boo-boo" and her mother or caregiver comes over to the crib and says, "Oh, you want your ba-ba?" and gets the child a favorite toy, the child soon learns that whenever she says, "ba-ba-boo-boo-ba-ba-boo-boo" a friendly face appears and gives her some attention. Therefore, what may start out as pre-intentional communication can quickly become intentional.

Let's look at another example. As a baby starts to develop her motor skills, she may stretch out her arms toward the sky. If she does this and an adult interprets this gesture as meaning the baby wants to be picked up, the behavior will eventually become intentional on the part of the baby.

These examples illustrate the importance of responding to any attempt by the child to communicate, whether or not the attempt is intentional. This is especially true of children with autism who often do not attempt to communicate intentionally. Intentional communication is quite different, however, from echolalia.

How Do I Start Helping a Child Communicate?

The best place to start is by observing the child until you have determined what methods or actions he uses to communicate and under what conditions he is most likely to communicate. In general terms, a child will communicate when:

◆ he is able to attend to what is being said.
◆ he is able to understand what is said by others.
◆ he experiences the responsiveness of others to his attempts at communication.
◆ he has a reason to communicate.

It is also important to find out what motivates a child. Look for reasons why he might or might not communicate. Learn to recognize that children with autism do not communicate in the same way as their peers. For example, if Kerry throws down her food when the teacher places it in front of her, she may be communicating that she does not want to eat. In this case, it would be helpful for her teacher and speech pathologist to work together to figure out an alternative way for her to communicate that she is not hungry. It will be necessary for the teacher and others who work with the child to determine her stage of communication. Trying to force a child to communicate before she is ready not only frustrates the child, but also it could delay her progress.

What Do You Mean by Stages of Communication?

The various stages of communication have been given a variety of names and defined in many different ways. For the purposes of this book, only those stages that preschool children might experience will be discussed. A speech pathologist can help you learn more about the traditional developmental stages of communication. The stages that most preschool children will experience have been condensed for this book and include:

◆   "It's all about me"—Egocentric Stage
◆   "I want it"—Requesting Stage
◆   Actions and reactions—Emerging Communication Stage
◆   Two-way street—Reciprocal Communication Stage

Egocentric Stage

The "It's All About Me" (egocentric) stage usually occurs in typically developing children when they are around two years old. Because children with autism may be delayed in their overall development, it is not uncommon for a child with autism to communicate in this stage when she arrives in your preschool classroom. Children in the egocentric stage might:

◆   reach their hands out to indicate "I want."
◆   scream or cry when they don't get something they want.
◆   smile or laugh when someone looks at them.
◆   be very shy around strangers.
◆   not interact with other children, but interact with adults who are familiar to them.
◆   experiment with how language sounds and say phrases repeatedly.

Requesting Stage

The "I want it" (requesting) stage occurs as the child learns cause and effect. He begins to understand that what he says or does has an effect on people or on his environment. During this stage, a child starts to see communication as a means to get what he wants.

Children in the requesting stage might:
◆   grab your hand and pull you toward something they want.
◆   say a few basic words.
◆   move their bodies when you are interacting with them to communicate "I want more."
◆   begin to sign the word "more," by putting their hands together.
◆   approximate words or attempt a few new words.

Communicating involves a partner.

Emerging Communication Stage

The child who functions in the emerging communication stage is beginning to use communication in a more functional manner. She is starting to understand that she can repeat the same action, gesture, or word and it gets the same result. Children in this stage will put two words together and seem to enjoy repeating what they just heard. The communication interactions that occur with the child are much longer and more sustained than in the previous stages.

Children in the emerging communication stage might:
◆ take turns.
◆ understand the names of those familiar to them.
◆ repeat what they just heard.
◆ use gestures more consistently, such as shaking their heads "no."
◆ answer simple questions.
◆ ask for something or request that you continue something.
◆ use words or signs in a more meaningful way.

Reciprocal Communication Stage

The "Two-Way Street" (reciprocal communication) stage is characterized by more direct communication with a partner. Often, children in this stage are more prone to communicate with an adult than with a peer. While children with autism continue to have difficulty with initiating or beginning conversations with peers, children at this stage may participate in a conversation if they have a strong need or a motivation to get something from the other child.

Children with autism rarely initiate spontaneous communication. If the child communicates, she still needs for conversations to be very concrete and literal. Steven Shore, a man with autism, recalls when he was a child, a peer said to him, "I feel like a pizza." Steven did not respond to the peer because he had no idea how a "pizza feels"—after all, pizzas don't have feelings. Children in this

114

stage of communication may have difficulty with social cues, new social situations, and understanding the abstracts of language, such as jokes. They also have difficulty understanding when someone is kidding them or making light of something. Children in the reciprocal communication stage might:

◆ intentionally use words to greet, ask for something, protest something, ask questions, and tell about something.

◆ express ideas and feelings that are relevant to them.

◆ have short conversations (although children with autism will always be more easily distracted than their peers).

◆ repeat something, if they think the listener does not understand.

◆ start to use longer sentences with more descriptive words.

How Do I Set Appropriate Goals for Communication?

It is difficult to know which goals to set when a child is learning to communicate. It is equally challenging to know what to expect from a child with autism, especially at the preschool level. While each child is unique and will communicate in his own way, there are several general suggestions to think about when setting communication goals.

Communication is most effective when it involves interaction with others. Learning to interact with other people is a life skill that the child can build on and use throughout his life.

In order to communicate effectively, the child must have a reliable form or way to communicate. During the preschool years, it is important to help the child use a form that will enable him to interact with his peers.

The ultimate goal for any child is to learn to communicate because it is meaningful to him. You want the child with autism to learn to do more than just tell you what he wants and needs; you want him to learn to use communication as a form of self-expression.

Communication should be meaningful. Help the child learn to communicate a way to connect his world with that of his peers.

In addition to the general guidelines above, the communication goals found in Table 6-2 (see page 118) are based on the child's stage of communication.

The ultimate goal for any child is to learn to communicate because it is meaningful to him…to learn to do more than just tell you what he wants and needs…

Table 6-2: Communication Goals

Stage of Communication	Goals
Egocentric	◆ "Nothing is free"—Require the child to show you what he wants by pointing, gesturing, or using sign language. ◆ Play simple games that involve taking turns, such as rolling a ball back and forth. Verbalize what you are doing. Say, "It is my turn" and point to yourself, then say, "It is your turn" and point to the child. ◆ Consistently respond to every communication attempt, even if it is unintentional. Verbalize what the child is doing.
Requesting	◆ Play a game or start an activity. Then, stop and try to get the child to request "more," either by moving his body or looking at you. ◆ When the child pulls you toward something or points to a desired object, respond. Then, verbalize what he wanted and say the name of the object. ◆ Describe everything the child does. Remember to use simple sentences. ◆ Children with autism often respond poorly to continuous talk. They are under-responsive to verbal stimuli. Provide a model. Say it from the child's point of view. Wait expectantly, and show rather than say often.
Emerging Communication	◆ Continue to play games that involve taking turns, but encourage the child to play with other children. ◆ Provide an exact model of what you want the child to say and do. ◆ Respond to any situations where the child initiates a communication interaction. ◆ Build on the child's expanding vocabulary by giving him experiences that will help him develop new words. ◆ If the child is using pictures to communicate, try to encourage him to use words, too.
Reciprocal Stage	◆ Set up classroom situations that encourage conversation. ◆ Throughout all stages, the environment plays a major role in helping children interact. ◆ Play games where you practice the rules of conversation, such as starting, stopping, and waiting for a turn. ◆ Help the child use communication for more than just simple requests. Talk about communicating feelings or opinions. ◆ Ask other children in the classroom to be peer buddies and talk with the child.

Should I Stop Trying to Make Her Talk and Use an Alternative Form of Communication?

Friends use pictures to communicate.

While learning to talk is always important, it may not be possible for all children. For children with autism, what is most important is that they communicate with purpose. Usually, when a child is not using words or word-like noises to request items, doesn't comment about things, or respond to questions, it is time to consider using an alternative way to communicate. Just because a child learns to use an alternative form of communication does not necessarily mean she will never learn to speak. It may mean that she needs a bridge or a way to help her as she learns to speak.

An alternative communication system is generally a method of communication that does not involve speech. Some children who remain nonverbal may ultimately use devices that speak for them. However, for most nonverbal preschool children, a more functional system will include either sign language or pictures. Even if the child is starting to use speech, sign language and/or pictures can be used to supplement her communication and facilitate comprehension and organization. They can also reduce the frustration she feels when she is unable to let people in her world know what she wants. Remember, children with autism are predominately strong visual learners and visual communication systems allow more understanding of the child's environment and facilitate expression.

Numerous studies have shown the use of alternative communication aides, like visual symbols, does not keep a child who may develop speech from talking. Rather, these studies show that communication supports help children, and enhance the ability of children who do develop spoken language to do so more effectively. Children with an IFSP or an IEP will have their communication needs addressed in their goals and objectives. However, these goals and objectives may not specify which communication system will work best for that child. It is important that everyone work together to understand and support the communication system that is most beneficial to the individual child.

Approximated sign for "more"

When and How Is the Best Way to Use Sign Language?

Sign language serves as a method of helping a child with autism communicate with the people in his world. Unfortunately, sign language is not universal and many people don't know even basic signs. In addition, some children don't have the motor skills to make signs and therefore approximate the sign or make one up on their own. This too, can be effective, if the teacher recognizes and understands the approximated signs. So, sign language can be a valuable tool that you can use to help children learn to communicate. If you and the child's family have decided to use basic signs with him, it is always a good idea to make a list of the signs, as he learns them, so others in his world will be able to communicate with him. Learning signs can become a game that all the children in your class enjoy.

Deciding which signs to teach first can be difficult. However, think about what three signs might help the child most in his environment. For example, the signs—*want*, *more*, and *all done* (finished) represent things that the child might use frequently throughout the day. (For more information about teaching sign language see page 124.) These three signs seem to be the starting place for most children, as they communicate many of the basic things for a child, and can be used in a variety of settings, including snack, meals, play, and so on. Table 6-3 includes pictures of some of the most commonly used signs.

Table 6-3: Commonly Used Signs

Word	Sign	Word	Sign
eat		drink	
inside		outside	
more		thank you	

Remember, just because a child begins to use signs to communicate does not necessarily mean he will always use signs. But whether sign language is a bridge to using more traditional forms of communication or a method that the child will use throughout his life, it will enable him to let others know what he wants and needs.

How Can a Child With Autism Use Pictures to Communicate?

Pictures are clearly more universal than sign language. Anyone, including a child's peer, can see if he points to a picture of a toy that means he would like to play with the toy. Handing a picture to a communication partner is one way that the child can interact with that partner. Pictures are used in various ways to make communication boards and embedded schedules, which can be combined to describe concepts and ideas. With pictures, a child can indicate a choice, a preference, or answer a question.

The most widely recognized formal system of communication is the Picture Exchange System (PECS), developed by Andy Bondy and Lori Frost. PECS can be purchased from Pyramid Education Products Inc. (http://www.pyramidproducts.com). In the PECS system, a child presents pictures to a partner or selects pictures from a board or portable notebook. The pictures are inexpensive and portable, allowing the child to use them in a variety of different situations. While pictures are an excellent teaching tool for children with autism, using the official PECS system requires special training, as there is a very specific method to presenting each sequence of pictures.

Pictures are great teaching tools, are practical, and easy to use, and also provide the opportunity for the child to use the same set of pictures at home or in his community. When using a picture communication system you will want to use the following guidelines:

- Help children become aware of how pictures can be used. Post picture schedules and refer to them often throughout the day. Use them to explain the sequence of an activity. Whenever you introduce a new word, hold up the picture. Children without autism may benefit from the added cues that pictures provide.
- The ultimate goal in using a picture system is to teach children to initiate communication. Once the child becomes more familiar with the pictures in the classroom, try to encourage him to use them to start a communication interaction.
- Build a list of commonly used pictures and practice with the child. Send pictures home and encourage the child's family to use them, too.
- Expand the picture list and ask questions that require the child to answer you by pointing to a picture.
- As the child becomes more comfortable with using the picture communication system, expand the pictures to include action pictures and pictures that can be used to tell you what and how the child is feeling.

HOW TO USE A PICTURE SYSTEM

- Help the children become aware of how pictures can be used.
- Encourage the children to use the pictures to start a communication interaction.
- Build a list of commonly used pictures and practice with the child.
- Send pictures home and encourage the child's family to use them.
- Expand the picture list and ask questions that require the child to answer you by pointing to a picture.
- Expand the pictures to include action pictures and pictures that can be used to tell you what and how the child is feeling.

For children who have difficulty understanding that the black and white drawings represent objects or concepts, other types of pictures can be used. For example, color photos are used in the SquarePics® Custom Cards Program. These photos represent objects and can be used in much the same way as described above.

What About Electronic Communication Devices?

Augmentative device helps a child communicate

While there are a few electronic communication devices simple enough for a young child to learn to use, young children usually do not use electronic communication devices. These devices are designed to provide a source of communication, specifically speech, but often they are they are often too expensive or too complex for a young child to use. However, if a child comes into your classroom with an electronic device, there are guidelines to consider:

◆ Be sure that the voice recorded on the device is a child's voice, not the voice of an adult.

◆ Contact the manufacturer of the device. Most manufacturers are happy to provide a free demonstration for teachers or, at the very least, provide materials about how the device works.

◆ Remember that the device belongs to the child. It is her voice and is not a toy to be used by other children.

◆ Find out what size batteries the device uses and keep plenty on hand.

Single message switches, such as the Big-Mack Jellybean Switch by AbleNet, Inc., are sometimes used to help children as they begin to communicate. It is a button type switch on which a single message has been recorded. The child is taught to push the button and the message is spoken. Unlike more expensive devices, this switch can be used with multiple children and is often a great tool when children are learning to let you know they need to go to the bathroom. A picture of a bathroom or a toilet can easily be taped or attached to the switch. Whenever any child needs to go, they just walk up to the switch and push the button. This device can be a great communication starter or a tool to use when you want to encourage participation. The message is easily changed and the device is easy to operate.

Communication is a lifelong learning skill that facilitates social relationships and helps the child relate to his environment. Regardless of how much or how little a child communicates, he will benefit from teachers who understand the following:

◆ how to encourage interaction,

◆ how he communicates best,

◆ why he communicates, and

◆ how to model language.

Introduce games that encourage communication.

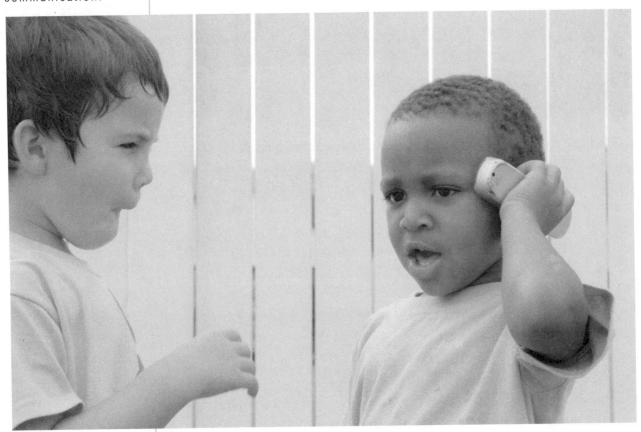

A Reason to Communicate

These activities include requiring the child to request, protest, and/or comment on what is going on. The more effectively you can engineer activities to allow children to do these things, the greater the likelihood that the communication will become intentional.

Strategy

What to Do

1. To facilitate a request, place a desired object slightly out of the child's reach. Wait, and briefly pretend that you don't know what he wants. If the child makes any attempt to request the item (gesture, sign, and so on), hand it to him and say, "Oh, you wanted the _____."

2. Another way to encourage the child to request an object is to place a desired item in a container that the child cannot open. He then must gesture, sign, or indicate what he wants you to do.

3. To further encourage the child to tell you what he wants, pretend you don't know, and see if he will persist in trying to tell you or show you what he wants.

4. To encourage the child to protest, hand him the wrong item or object and look at him as if you don't know what he wants. Do not frustrate him. Try to encourage the rule that "Nothing is free!" You must ask, gesture, or sign to get what you want.

5. Deliberately say or do something in the daily routine that is wrong. Sometimes children with autism will feel a compulsion to correct your mistake. This can lead to a more functional use of language.

Helpful Hints

◆ Tell others what you are doing, so they will know you are trying to get the child to communicate.

◆ Play a game with children—tell them ahead of time that you will be doing something wrong and they must be a detective and find out what it is.

◆ Model with all the children in your classroom that to get what they want, it will be a requirement that they request it in some way.

Objective

To encourage the child to have a reason to communicate

When to Use This Strategy

When you want to give the child a reason to communicate

Materials Needed

None

Three Basic Signs

Remember to work closely with all the adults who interact with the child so that they will use signs consistently, too.

Strategy (vertical tab)

Objective

To teach the child three basic signs: *thank you, more,* and *all done*

When to Use This Strategy

When the child is ready to learn a few basic signs

Materials Needed

None

What to Do

1. Getting ready to teach basic signs requires that the teacher is familiar with the signs and can make them correctly. Table 6-4 shows the correct way to make each of the three signs.

Table 6-4: Three Basic Signs

Thank You	More	All done (finished)

2. Practice the signs before you begin to use them with the child.
3. Remember that other children in your class may also benefit from using signs to communicate, so use the signs with the entire class.
4. Sign to yourself in the mirror. Once you are confident that you know the three basic signs, begin to use them in the class.
5. Always say the word as you sign.
6. Don't force a child to use the signs. Simply model each sign as you use it.
7. Praise the child for any attempt to imitate the sign.
8. After the child is familiar with the three basic signs, it is time to encourage her to use them. Encourage the child to let you know when she wants more and when she is finished.

Helpful Hints

◆ Making learning the signs a game that all the children can play.
◆ Encourage children in the class to use the signs with the child.
◆ Send home details about what and why you are teaching the three basic signs to the child. Parents who may be initially resistant to the use of sign language are often more open to the idea when they understand why you are doing it.

What Is It? Using Pictures to Identify Objects

Although a child with autism may know certain vocabulary words, he may not understand how to use speech to communicate.

What to Do

1. Select 10 pictures that you want to use with the child. Make sure the pictures clearly represent one specific item or activity.

2. Select pictures that are functional for the child and easily accessible in the classroom.

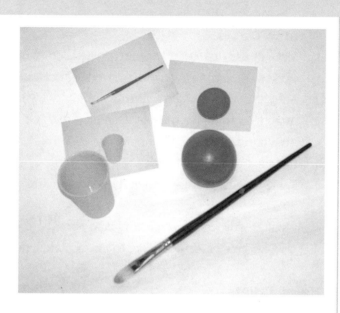

3. Start with pictures that you can use with real objects. For example, a cup, ball, book, paintbrush, and so on.

4. Pick up the object and the picture. Hand the object to the child. If he will not take it, try to direct his attention to the object. To help the child make the transition from pictures to objects, try putting the objects in small re-sealable sandwich bags for easy use and handling.

5. Point to the picture and say the word.

6. Start with 1 or 2 pictures and build up to 10.

7. Remember that the purpose of this activity is to help the child make the connection between the picture and the object.

Helpful Hints

♦ The child's attention span may be short, so make this activity short.

♦ Review the pictures throughout the day.

♦ Try to make this activity a game. The sooner he figures out that pictures can help him communicate better, the easier it will be for you.

♦ Don't forget to work with his parents and other caregivers, so that they are reinforcing what you are doing at school. The more often he sees the pictures, the easier it will be for him to use them.

Objective

To teach the child with autism to use pictures to identify objects

When to Use This Strategy

When you want to teach a child to use pictures and when you want him to understand that the pictures are symbols representing real objects

Materials Needed

10 pictures that represent a specific item or activity (avoid pictures with a lot of detail)—black and white line drawings usually work best; and 10 objects that match each picture

Strategy

Communication Apron

Start off with only a few cards attached to the apron. More can be added later.

Objective

To make communication pictures more readily accessible

When to Use This Strategy

When you are beginning to introduce pictures or when you want to make it easy for the child to see pictures during an activity

Materials Needed

A plastic craft apron or vinyl bib apron, sticky-back Velcro, communication pictures

What to Do

1. Make or use an existing apron. A plastic craft apron or a vinyl bib apron works best, although a solid colored vest can be used.
2. Attach sticky-back Velcro to the apron.
3. Attach Velcro to the back of each picture to be used.
4. Attach the pictures to the apron or vest. This provides an opportunity for the child to use language.
5. Remove the pictures when you need them and replace them when you have finished.
6. An alternative is to use clear plastic pockets to store the cards. The plastic pockets hold cards and more than one card can be placed in each pocket.

Helpful Hints

- Make sure the cards are large enough for the child to see.
- Move beyond things—use pictures that show an action or activity that the child will do.
- Use the cards as cues for other children who are having trouble with language concepts.

Guidelines for Picture Schedules

Even after the child has learned the daily routine, the picture schedule helps him feel that the day is organized and predictable.

What to Do

1. Decide how you want to display the schedule. Select a place that is easily accessible by the child. Remember to keep the schedule in the same location. You can have mini-picture schedule(s) posted throughout the room at each center, but there should always be one location for the master schedule.

2. Decide how you will post the schedule. Clear plastic holders work best. Try using a hanging shoe bag with clear plastic pockets or purchasing clear pockets with a sticky back. These can be found at most office supply stores.

Center Time   Cleanup   Compu

3. Make sure the pictures are sturdy enough to handle frequently. Laminating, if possible, helps to preserve them.

4. The pictures must not be too small. The minimum size should be 2" x 2".

5. After the child has learned the schedule, you can expand it.

Helpful Hints

◆ Refer to the schedule often throughout the day and use it with all the children in the classroom.

◆ Use the schedule to let the child know what will happen next.

◆ When the schedule is going to change, be sure to change the schedule cards as well.

◆ Make sure all the adults who work with the child use the schedule to help him know what will be occurring.

Objective

To help the child understand what will happen in the daily routine and/or how to carry out the steps within a daily routine

When to Use This Strategy

When you want to teach the child about what is going to happen next

Materials Needed

Pictures and clear holders, such as a clear, plastic shoe rack or a surface on which pictures can easily be removed and changed as necessary

Sing to Me: Using Music to Communicate

Many times a child with autism will sing when she might not be as open to a conversation.

Strategy

Objective

To use familiar songs and rhymes, help make communication fun, and learn new vocabulary

When to Use This Strategy

When you have observed the child and determined that the child responds well to music. This strategy is also a way to encourage interaction.

Materials Needed

None

What to Do

1. Choose simple songs with tunes the child recognizes. Songs with repeating words often work best.
2. Sing about activities or things that the child enjoys.
3. Stress key words, concepts, or vocabulary.
4. Don't be concerned if you can't sing well; it's the interaction that children find enjoyable.
5. Use the child's name whenever possible.
6. Consider the following examples.

New Foods

A *song to encourage eating*
(sung to the tune of "Mary Had a Little Lamb")

Mark is eating peas today, peas today, peas today,
Mark is eating peas today, I am so glad.

Or

_____ (child's name) *is trying* _____ (name of new food) *today,* _____ (name of new food) *today,* _____ (name of new food) *today,* _____ (child's name) *is trying* _____ (name of new food) *today, I am so glad.*

Play With Me!

A *song to encourage playing together*
(sung to the tune of "Twinkle, Twinkle Little Star")

Won't you come and play with me?
We'll have fun just wait and see.
First it's your turn, then it's mine.
We'll be friends all the time.
Won't you come and play with me?
Well have fun just wait and see.

Sing to Me: Using Music to Communicate

An Action Song

A song to describe an action
(sung to the tune of "Row, Row, Row Your Boat")

Terrance has a bright blue car.
It's his favorite toy.
He will roll it up and down.
Terrance has a blue car.

My Friend

A song about how to treat others
(sung to the tune of "Old McDonald Had a Farm")

Tamika plays so well.
She is my friend.
She takes turns and shares her toys.
She is a friend.
She treats others very well.
She is a friend.
She helps put up all the toys.
She is a friend.

7. Once the child learns the song, leave out words and wait expectantly for the child to fill them in. She may use a word picture, sign, or gesture to fill in the missing part of the song.

Helpful Hints

◆ Involve other children in the class and encourage them to help you write songs.

◆ Sing in a pleasant tone, keeping in mind that loud noises can overwhelm a child with autism.

Puppets as Talking Partners

Children with autism will often talk with an inanimate object before they talk to a human.

Objective

To encourage communication and enhance make-believe play through puppets

When to Use This Strategy

When you want to encourage the child to communicate with you or when you want to enable the child to spontaneously interact with others

Materials Needed

A puppet

What to Do

1. To help the child get used to a puppet, introduce the puppet into the learning activity. For example, a mouse puppet could help the class with a simple rhyme like "Hickory, Dickory, Dock."

2. Talk for the puppet, using a funny animated voice.

3. Make the puppet nod, move its head, look over at the child, and then look away.

4. Smile, so that the child will understand this is a game.

5. Ask the child if he would like to hold the puppet.

6. If the child uses a pretend voice, continue to encourage him to talk to his classmates or talk to you and tell you what he is doing.

Helpful Hints

◆ If the child responds well to the puppet, add additional puppets.

◆ Expand the activity by encouraging the child to use puppets with a friend.

◆ Make a puppet theatre from a cardboard box, if desired.

Strategy

Communication Notebooks: Opportunities for Interaction

Communication notebooks are great tools to use to encourage children with autism to express their feelings.

Strategy

What to Do

1. Photo albums with individual pockets for pictures make great holders for the child's pictures. Wallets with fold-out plastic photo holders can also be used to make great picture stories.
2. To begin, take a single experience that the child has had and see if she will point to some pictures that tell you about what she saw, felt, or did.
3. You can prompt the child by providing hints and picture cues.
4. Write a sentence to go with each page in the book.
5. Communication books also can be used to help the child express her emotions.
6. Encourage the child to carry her communication book with her and refer to it whenever possible.

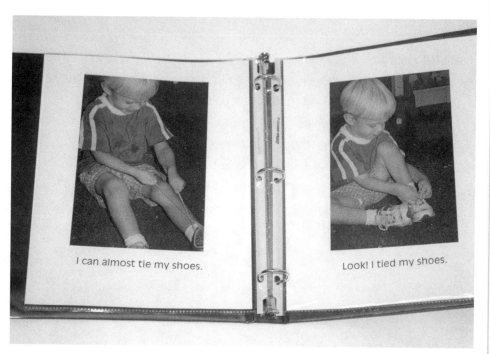

I can almost tie my shoes.

Look! I tied my shoes.

Objective

To help the child record her experiences and activities in a way that she can use to talk about things she has done or places she has visited. Communication notebooks also make great conversation starters.

When to Use This Strategy

When the child is beginning to use pictures to communicate and you have observed that she understands that pictures represent concepts and words

Materials Needed

Photo album or individual pocket pages with accompanying pictures

Helpful Hints

◆ Encourage parents to make communication books at home and send them to school. Knowing what the child enjoys at home can be very helpful when you are looking for conversation starters.

◆ Try using communication notebooks as problem solvers to help the child solve a problem or figure out how to do something.

Sentence Starters

This strategy also increases vocabulary and helps the child make longer sentences.

Objective

To expand the use of language and increase vocabulary

When to Use This Strategy

When the child is beginning to use a few words in a functional way

Materials Needed

None

What to Do

1. Develop a ritual or routine for teaching a new word or phrase. Each time you introduce a new word, do so in the same way. You might even have a set time during each day when you introduce a couple of new words to the child.
2. Begin, by saying the same words, "Look _____ (child's name), today we are going to learn about _____ (point to the object)."
3. Next say, "See? This is a _____ (say the name of the object or hold up a picture of the word).
4. Now say, "Let's say the name together. This is a _____."
5. "Let's say it again. This is a _____."
6. Ask, "What is this?" Then, pause and give the child time to answer.
7. Respond with, "That's right. It is a _____."

Helpful Hints

◆ Labeling is a good way to teach vocabulary, but it is not a good method for interaction. Avoid placing too many labels on things, as it will be overwhelming to the child.
◆ Expand the activity by adding adjectives that describe color or size.
◆ See if the child can make a sentence with the new words.
◆ Don't forget to review previously learned words.
◆ For words to have meaning, the child must have experiences to which he can connect the words. Be sure to use his new words and give him plenty of practice using the words in his daily activities.

Learning to Communicate "Yes" and "No!"

The sooner a child can let you know what she wants, the less likely she may be to have a tantrum because she feels no one understands her needs.

What to Do

1. Determine the most likely manner in which the child can be prompted to use the concept of yes/no. These might include: sign for yes/no, nodding or shaking the head, or saying it verbally.

2. Play a game where you ask the child yes/no questions. Begin with objects. For example, hold up a book and say, "Is this a book?"

3. Pause, and give the child time to answer.

4. As the child learns to respond, ask questions about people, such as, "Are you a girl?" or "Is this your daddy?"

5. Expand the activity to include questions about color, size, shape, and actions.

6. As the child begins to use yes/no more consistently, ask her questions about herself, such as, "Do you want to go to the art center?"

Helpful Hints

◆ Try this adaptation: Use two single-message switches like the Big-Mack Jellybean Switch discussed on page 121 of this chapter. On one switch, record the word "yes" and attach a picture that represents "yes" to the top of the switch, on the other switch record the word "no" and attach a picture of "no." The child can push the switch to answer the question.

◆ Expand the game to include questions that require the child to problem solve on a higher level, such as holding up a blue car and saying, "Is this a red car?"

Objective

To provide a way for the child to indicate her preferences and to help the child begin to answer simple questions

When to Use This Strategy

When the child is learning to request items or when you have determined that she is ready to start letting you know her preferences

Materials Needed

None

Resources Used in This Chapter

Bondy, A. & L. Frost. 2002. *A picture's worth*: PECS *and other visual communication strategies in autism*. Bethesda, MD: Woodbine House.

Gillingham, G. 2000. *Autism a new understanding*. Edmonton, Alberta, Canada: Tacit Publishing, Inc.

Johnson, M. D., & S.H. Corden. 2004. *Beyond words*: *the successful inclusion of a child with autism*. Knoxville, TN: Merry Pace Press.

Kluth, P. 2003. *You're going to love this kid!*: *Teaching students with autism in the inclusive classroom*. Baltimore: Paul H. Brookes Publishing Co.

Small, M. & L. Kontente. 2003. *Everyday solutions*: *A practical guide for families of children with autism spectrum disorders*. Shawnee Mission, KS: Autism Asperger Publishing Company.

Sonders, S.A. 2002. *Giggle time*: *Establishing the social connection*: *a program to develop the communication skills of children with autism, Asperger's Syndrome and PDD*. London: Jessica Kingsley Publishers Ltd.

Strock, M. 2004. *Autism spectrum disorders* (*Pervasive Developmental Disorders*). Bethesda, MD: National Institute of Mental Health, National Institutes of Health, U.S. Department of Health and Human Services. (NIH Publication No. NIH-04-5511)

Sussman, F. 1999. *More than words*: *Helping parents promote communication and social skills in young children with autism spectrum disorder*. Toronto: The Hanen Centre.

Key Terms

Alternative Communication System: A method of communication that does not involve speech.

Communication: An interaction between two or more people where information is exchanged.

Echolalia: The echoing and repetition of a phrase or word.

Electronic communication device: Sometimes called an augmentative communication device; a mechanical device that is designed to talk for the child, when it is activated either by a switch or by pressing a button.

Expressive communication: How the child inputs his message to the person receiving it. The method used to communicate with others.

Intentional communication: Communication that is on purpose or deliberate.

Language disorder: A deficit in using words or vocabulary. It can also involve how a child understands language and uses it in social settings.

Non-functional communication: Communication that lacks meaning or purpose.

Pragmatic language: Involves using language in a social setting. For example, knowing what is appropriate to say, when to say it, and the general give-and-take nature of a friendly conversation.

Receptive communication: How the child receives messages or information from others.

Inside **Their Own Worlds:**
Encouraging Children With Autism to Play

How Does the Play of Children With Autism Differ From Their Peers?

For most children, play is a valuable and fun way to learn. It helps a child develop relationships with others, learn how to solve problems, express emotions, and use his imagination to create new experiences and explore the world around him. Play is the main vehicle through which children learn to get along with others and socialize; it is how a child experiments and solves problems in his world.

New activities are fun.

135

Play, like other developmental milestones, develops as the child begins to experience new activities and explore new environments. The solitary play of a toddler, with experience, develops into the interactive, reciprocal play of a preschool age child.

While the stages of play have been described in many ways, most experts agree that typically developing children begin to explore their world by manipulating and experimenting with objects that interest them. Later, a child will become involved in a more functional type of play when she uses objects, such as placing a block on top of another block or putting a plastic spoon beside a bowl. As she develops cognitively, she may substitute one object for another, such as picking up a block and pretending it is a camera. This will lead to imaginative play or pretend play.

In summary, play:

◆ is a fun and joyful experience.

◆ requires that a child become an active participant.

◆ is a voluntary experience that comes from within.

◆ has no real agenda, except what the child wants it to be.

◆ requires that a child learn to use symbols, such as when a cardboard box becomes a jet plane.

◆ is the primary vehicle through which a child learns the rules of socialization.

Play involves active participation.

When considering the major characteristics of autism, it is understandable why children with autism do not follow a typical pattern when they play. Because many children with autism become obsessed with objects in non-typical ways and do not socialize easily, their play is not as socially interactive as that of their peers. In addition, when we consider the communication issues and marked disinterest they often show for the world around them, it is no wonder that encouraging children with autism to play with others can be very challenging. Although children with autism may manipulate objects or engage in some form of experimental play, it is usually very different from that of their peers. Children with autism are often very repetitive in their movements; this is also seen in their play.

While they tend to be somewhat involved with materials and objects that involve the senses, children with autism often show a marked preference for only one type of play material. For example, Sam will build a road for his cars but he only uses square blocks and he only plays with red cars. Also, since children with autism are usually very literal, they do not always understand or

Pretend or imaginative play

show any desire to participate in symbolic or pretend play. In addition, make-believe and imaginative play, especially if it involves role play or interaction with others, is very uncommon. For example, if asked to use sequence cards to retell the story of The Three Little Pigs, Shondra will gladly comply. However, when you ask several children to reenact the story, Shondra stares at the ceiling as if she does not understand what is being asked of her.

It is very difficult for the child with autism to understand the social relationships involved in playing successfully with others. Even if they are interested in such interaction, most children with autism do not know how to engage themselves in a play activity with someone else. For this reason, they become even more socially isolated. While their peers are learning to build relationships in play groups and play activities, they are often left sitting alone, absorbed in a favorite toy. Jerome, for example, enjoys making a collage out of bits of fabric, string, and colored paper. However, if you ask him to make a kite with a peer, he turns his back on you and walks away.

What Can I Do to Encourage Children to Play?

Before you can encourage play, it is important to spend some time observing the child. Use Table 7-1 (see page 140) to make notes that will help you determine what interests the child most. Structuring play around his interests will greatly increase the chances of positive play interactions and will make him more likely to show an interest in what is going on.

When we consider the communication issues and marked disinterest autistic children often show for the world around them, it is no wonder that encouraging them to play with others can be very challenging.

Table 7-1: Play Observations

Questions to Ask	How Does the Child Play?	Examples You Observe
Does he prefer a toy or an object?	◆ What does he do with it? ◆ Does he play? ◆ Does he just watch while it moves? ◆ Does he just sit and stare at the object?	
What activity does he seem to repeat?	◆ How does he act when he is repeating the activity? ◆ Does it have more than one step? ◆ Will he let others engage in the activity with him?	
What materials does he use most often?	◆ Is his preference for color or size? ◆ Does he prefer one texture over another? ◆ How does he respond when you introduce something new, such as a new toy?	
What does he do when he plays with an object or toy?	◆ Will he engage in multiple activities with the same toy? ◆ Will he let others share the toy with him? ◆ Does he play appropriately with the toy or does he just repeat a movement over and over?	
Does he have a collection or need to have an object with him when he plays?	◆ Will he put aside his desired object when something new is introduced?	
If he does engage in pretend play, is there a theme he prefers?	◆ Does he use the same theme (pretending to be a doctor or a firefighter) every time he plays? ◆ Will he assign themes to other activities?	
Does he play with others? Who?	◆ If he does play with others, who does he play with most? ◆ Will he play with other children or just adults? ◆ How does he react when you bring over a new peer buddy to play with him?	

How Do I Use What I Have Observed?

Once you have observed how a child plays and what she prefers to play with, it will be easier to plan activities that focus on her interests. Make sure the child has time to play with preferred objects and is not under stress to stop or share the toy until she is ready. Once the child has played with the preferred item for a few minutes, try to encourage her to try something new by putting the new toy beside her and walking away. Don't take away the preferred toy but, after a few minutes, return and ask if she would like to play with the new toy.

Another way to help teach the child to play with others is to ask a peer to help. However, it is important that you select a peer buddy who recognizes that, while the child is different in the way she responds, she can still be fun to play with.

How Do I Select an Appropriate Peer Buddy?

A peer buddy is a volunteer who agrees to play with the child for a given time. Observe the other children in your class and try to determine who has interests that are similar to that of the child with autism. Next, look at individual characteristics. Which child might be more tolerant of a peer with autism? Who seems to be more patient with others? Who might be willing to play with the child, even if the child has rejected him as a friend in the past? For younger preschoolers, try to find a peer buddy who is four or five years old.

Peer buddies play together.

You may be able to identify a peer buddy immediately, and you can begin to train him in the procedures you have set up for the child. At other times, you may have to be more creative and look outside your classroom for a first-time peer buddy. Maybe there is an older child in another classroom who can visit your class and be a peer buddy for a little while each day, or if your program has after-school care, there may be a school-age child who can play with the child with autism.

Some teachers put "help-wanted" posters in their classroom and ask children to apply for classroom jobs. If you put up a help-wanted poster for a peer buddy, be sure to put up other help-wanted posters for other classroom jobs, so that all children in the class have the opportunity to apply for a classroom position. This technique is also very effective for children with autism, as they can learn to apply for a classroom job that interests them.

After you have selected the right peer buddy, you can begin helping the child with autism to play more effectively with others. The first step in this process is to look at the steps involved in learning to play with others.

How Do I Begin to Teach This Process?

Begin the process by interviewing the peer buddy and explaining that, for the next few days, you will need his help in playing with the child with autism. Remember to use the child's name, such as, "Brandon, thank you so much for volunteering to be a peer buddy for Kimberly. Every day, I will tell you what I need for you to do to help Kimberly learn to play."

Sharing play space takes practice.

Next, invite the peer buddy to play beside the child for a few minutes. Do not encourage them to play together or to communicate. If that happens, great! But, at this point, you are trying to get the child with autism to accept someone else in her space. She must be willing to do this, before any type of cooperative play is possible. While you may not be able to teach a child with autism to make friends in the traditional sense, you may be able to orchestrate some situations that encourage positive interactions. However, first, you must teach her to tolerate the presence of other children. Accepting the presence of others in her personal space is an important step in learning to play with peers.

After the peer buddy has played in the child's space for a few minutes, ask him to leave the area. It is important to gradually introduce children with autism to the presence of others. Later in the day (or the following day), ask the same peer to help again. This time, encourage him to play beside his friend with autism for a little longer. Continue this process for several days, before you start encouraging the children to share the same toys. After the child has learned to tolerate a peer and share the same toys, it is time to gradually introduce activities that will encourage the children to interact.

If the child is communicating with simple signs or using a communication device, teach the peer buddy how to talk to the child using that form of communication. Even if it is nothing more than making the sign for "want" or "more," it can be the first step to a positive play experience for both children.

Ideas and Activities for Encouraging Children to Play

When trying to encourage a child with autism to play, keep the following points in mind:

◆ Focus on the interests of the child.

◆ Make interactions with others as natural as possible.

◆ Recognize that children with autism may have difficulty adjusting to new play situations and new play materials.

◆ Explain activities that involve more than one step and provide picture cues to help the child know what to do next.

◆ Allow the child to leave a play activity, if it becomes overwhelming.

◆ Honor the child's need to play alone; some preschool children with autism aren't ready to play in large groups. That is why learning centers are effective with preschool children, as they afford them the choice to work alone or in small groups.

◆ Avoid upsetting the child; let her know ahead of time that it will soon be time to stop playing, so that she has time to accept that there will be a change.

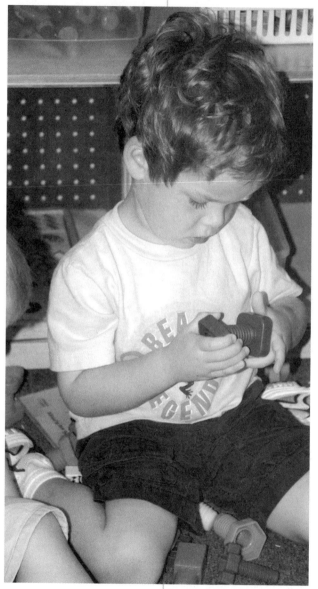

Structure play around the interests of the child.

Solitary play

General Suggestions for Teaching Play Strategies

Before selecting a strategy to help you encourage play, it is important to remember the following general suggestions:

- Introduce one new toy or activity at a time. Too much change can be overwhelming.

- If you are teaching the child to do something for the first time, break it down into a few simple steps.

- Show him each step. Then, ask him to repeat it after you.

- Start off with very short periods of structured play. Then, make the time longer as the child learns to tolerate the activity.

- Talk about the activity. Be animated and use a happy approach by saying such things as, "Wow, I just love rolling the ball to you!" or, "You built that tower so high, isn't this fun?"

- If the child is prone to a self-stimulatory activity, such as hand flapping or hitting himself, try to find an activity that requires him to use his hands in other ways.

- When teaching a new skill, use the child's name and tell him what will happen.

- Next, show him or model the steps in the activity, and encourage the child to try the activity on his own.

- Make sure every play activity is fun and rewarding for the child. Remember, the main reason children play is because it is fun!

Give and Take—Learning Reciprocity

Initially, this strategy involves just you and the child; later, it can be expanded to include other children. This strategy works best when the child is relaxed.

What to Do

1. Sit facing the child. You will need to sit close to her. Later, as she learns what to do, you can move back.

2. Hold up the item you want to exchange (ball, car, doll, and so on). Make sure the toy is in the child's line of vision. Smile and show lots of interest in the toy.

3. Use the child's name and the toy's name in a sentence. For example, "Sarah look, Miss Lynne has a doll."

4. Repeat Step 3 until the child glances at the doll. When she does, look at the doll and place it in her hand.

5. Identify the doll as the child's. For example, say, "Sarah's doll," pause, and see if the child will hold the doll.

6. Gently take the doll back, and say, "Miss Lynne's doll." Place your free hand on your chest and gently tap it a couple of times as a cue that says, "mine."

7. Repeat the process, using the same words each time. Remember to pause to give the child an opportunity to take the doll.

8. After a few times of taking the doll back, wait, and extend your hand, to see if the child will place the doll into your hand.

Helpful Hints

◆ Be aware that it may take many tries before the child begins to hand you the item without your having to take it back.

◆ Once the child has become accustomed to the routine, try using other toys. This encourages the child to generalize what she has learned to other objects.

◆ After the child is familiar with what to do, sit further and further away from her. When you are confident that she understands how to exchange a toy in a playful way, ask another peer to join in and try the activity with her.

Objective

To help the child participate in a basic give-and-take game with another person

When to Use This Strategy

When the child is ready to learn about reciprocity with another person

Materials Needed

Small hand-held toy, such as a ball or car

Strategy

Strategy

Which Toy Should I Use?

If you know the child has difficulty sharing, have more than one item of the same kind available.

Objective

To help determine which toys to use based on the child's preferences and needs

When to Use This Strategy

When you want to determine which toy might be the most effective to introduce to a specific child

Materials Needed

Classroom toys

What to Do

1. Consider the age of the child, his social development, and how well he communicates with others
2. Select a toy based on the child's development and needs as well as your goals and objectives for him.
3. Use Table 7-2 as general guidelines for selecting toys.

Table 7-2: Guidelines for Selecting Toys

Type and General Purpose of Toy	Examples
Cause-and-effect toys or toys that require an action by the child, such as pushing a button or pulling a lever	Jack-in-the-box Flashlight Simple switch-operated toys such as a tape recorder See-N-Say toys
Toys that are related to visual-tape recorder	Puzzles with knobs Stacking rings Nesting cups Shape-sorting toys
Toys that aid in construction or building	Blocks of various shapes and sizes Building toys, such as Legos™ Stringing beads Snap-together toys
Toys that encourage reciprocity (the exchange between two people)	Small hand-held toys such as balls Blowing bubbles Small moving toys such as cars, trucks, and airplanes
Sensory materials that encourage creativity	Art materials, paint, glue, scraps of cloth or paper, art paper, crayons String or yarn
"Let's pretend" toys	Puppets Realistic-looking toys that represent things such as food, clothes, and so on Dress-up clothes including hats, shoes, and jewelry

Which Toy Should I Use?

4. Trial-and-error can be the best tool. Introduce a toy and see if the child seems to take an interest in it. If he does not, try something else.

5. Be creative; sometimes a large box can quickly become a wonderful pretend airplane or a tunnel.

6. Because some children with autism enjoy crawling in and around things, try making a simple obstacle course out of classroom materials, such as chairs, tables, or large therapy balls.

Helpful Hints

◆ Your agenda and the child's preferences may not match. Be flexible enough to change your plans if the child wants to do something else.

◆ As the child begins to communicate more, introduce games with rules. Start with matching games and move up to more traditional games such as Candyland or Hi-Ho! Cherry–O.

Strategy

It's My Space—A Strategy to Encourage Children to Play Side by Side

Keep in mind that many children with autism will never be able to tolerate large numbers of children in their play space.

Objective

To encourage children to tolerate the presence of other children in their play space and to encourage parallel play

When to Use This Strategy

When you have observed the child and determined that he plays alone for an extended period and will tolerate the presence of others

Materials Needed

Two or three of the child's favorite or preferred toys

What to Do

1. Make sure the play area has clearly defined boundaries, such as shelves or an area rug.

2. Allow the child to spend time in the play area alone, before introducing another child into the area.

3. Place one or two toys nearby that the child enjoys playing with.

4. After he has played for a few minutes, put a few toys nearby that his peers enjoy playing with.

5. Ask one or more children to play in the same area as the child with autism, but instruct them to play with the toys you have put there for them. Use the child's name and say, "_____ is playing alone right now. Would you like to play next to him?"

6. Select toys for peers that can easily be shared, if the two children decide to play together. Examples might include blocks, art supplies, or toys with wheels, such as cars and trucks.

Accepting the presence of others is important

It's My Space—A Strategy to Encourage Children to Play Side by Side

7. Do not interrupt the children while they are playing unless the child with autism becomes upset and reacts. When they have finished, gently and softly make a statement that lets him know you are pleased that he let his peer play beside him. For example, "Michael, thank you for letting Latisha play with you today."

8. As the child begins to tolerate others in his play space, introduce more toys and more children to the play area.

Helpful Hints

◆ A crowded, disorganized play area may be very confusing to the child, especially if he likes things neatly arranged in specific places.

◆ Be sure that you put the play materials in the same place on the same shelf every day, because routine is very important to children with autism.

◆ Visual drawings or picture cues make it easier for a child with autism to know where a specific toy is located.

◆ Some children function better when toys are placed in plastic bins rather than placed randomly on a shelf.

Strategy

Paper Sack Game—What Did You Find?

Be sure to explain that this is just a game, and assure the child that he does not have to look into or reach into the sack.

Objective

To encourage natural curiosity and provide opportunities for structured interaction with peers

When to Use This Strategy

When you want to encourage the child's natural curiosity

Materials Needed

A brown paper sack and four or five items from the classroom, such as a small ball, a piece of yarn, a crayon, a rock, a plastic spoon, soft material, or a cotton ball

What to Do

1. Explain that you are going to play a guessing game.
2. Tell the children that each child will have a turn to reach into the sack and guess what is inside. Be sure to put one item in at a time.
3. Ask the first child to reach inside and feel the item. Let each child have a turn before anyone guesses what is inside.
4. Vary the game by asking the child to describe what is inside without naming it.
5. After the child has described what he feels, ask if anyone in the group wants to guess what is inside the sack.
6. Later, after the children are more familiar with the game, let one person be "it." The other children will close their eyes while "it" goes around the room and selects a small item to place inside the paper sack. Then, the other children can open their eyes and reach inside to feel what is hidden there.

Helpful Hints

◆ Paper sacks are very flimsy. If possible, make a feely box to use, instead of a sack.

◆ If a child is hesitant to be "it," encourage him to choose a friend and they can be "it" together.

◆ Only play the game as long as the children are interested. Once they start to get tired, discontinue the game and go on to another activity.

◆ Remember that children with autism often do not like to touch certain textures. Use items that you know will be pleasant for the child with autism to touch and explore.

148

The Basics of Simple Games—Learning About Rules

Keep rules simple, and use language children understand.

What to Do

1. Introduce group rules to a few children at the same time. Explain that these rules will be posted with pictures so that everyone can see them when they are playing.

2. Limit the play group rules to just a few, and decide ahead of time what your rules will be. For example, with three-year-olds, the following rules can be useful:

   ◆ Be nice to everyone.
   ◆ Be gentle with toys.

   For older children, expand the rules to include such things as:

   ◆ Ask for help.
   ◆ Put toys away when you are finished.

3. Once you have established group play rules, post them in the play area. Use pictures whenever possible.

4. Review the rules often and refer to them each day, before the children begin to play.

5. The first few times you introduce the rules, model each one for the children and ask them to follow the rule with you.

6. If a child forgets a rule, take her over to the rule list and go over just the rule that she forgot to use.

7. Make going over the rules part of the daily routine, so that children learn to expect it as something that is done before they enter the play area.

Helpful Hints

◆ Make sure the rules are stated in a proactive and positive way.
◆ Refer to the pictures and explain clearly what each rule and each picture means.
◆ Be sure the rules are posted at the child's eye level.

Objective

To help children understand basic social rules for playing in small groups or for playing with others

When to Use This Strategy

When children are beginning to show an interest in playing with others or before you are going to introduce a small group activity that requires children to work or play together

Materials Needed

Cards or posters with the play group rules pictured on them

Same Old, Same Old, Same Old—Introducing a New Toy

Use this strategy when the child is relaxed and having fun. It is less effective when the child is over-stimulated by the environment and when he is tired.

Objective

To introduce a new toy or activity

When to Use This Strategy

When you have observed the child and determined he is ready for something new

Materials Needed

A new toy that you want to introduce to the child

What to Do

1. Before the child becomes involved in the activity, place the new toy on a table and cover it loosely with a piece of cloth.

2. Tell the child that you have hidden something under the cloth on the table and you want to see if he can figure out what it is.

3. Sit down with the child in front of the hidden toy. Lightly touch the toy without removing the blanket. Make a comment, such as, "Hmmm… this feels soft" or "Listen, I think this toy makes a noise."

4. Encourage the child to explore the toy without looking under the cloth.

5. Continue to explore the toy. Say things like, "Do you think it is a _____?"

6. After a few minutes, ask the child to guess what is hidden under the cloth. Pause, and wait for him to answer.

7. Lift the cloth with the child and say, "Oh look, it is a _____ (fill in the name of the toy)."

Helpful Hints

◆ Children with autism are often hesitant to explore new toys. Think of creative ways to get their attention directed to the new toy.

◆ After you have uncovered the toy, ask the child to play with it or ask him to take it to the center where it belongs.

◆ Initially, use a toy that you know will interest the child. Later, you can try the same activity with a toy that may not be preferred by the child.

Scarf Dance

This strategy works best in a small-group setting. It is also important to have plenty of space for the children to move around. Make sure the children know where the designated space for this activity is, such as on the carpet in a particular area of the room.

What to Do

1. Smile and hold up your scarf. Tell the children you are going to play a game where they wave their scarves and move to the music.

2. Tell the children you will show them how to play the game. Play the music and gently move around, while waving your scarf in time to the music.

3. Hand each child a scarf and let him practice waving the scarf to music.

4. Tell the children that when the music stops, they must stop in place until the music starts again. Practice and model this step several times.

5. Initially, stop the music very soon after you start it. Later, wait longer before stopping the music.

6. Continue to model the game until the child with autism understands what to do. If he seems confused, stand next to him and gently guide him as the music plays.

Helpful Hints

◆ Avoid using the words *freeze in place*, as they are abstract and may be very confusing for the child.

◆ Experiment with different types of music to see which one works best.

◆ A variation of this game is to use art supplies and encourage children to paint or draw to the music, stopping when the music stops.

Objective

To encourage the child to participate in a movement game with music

When to Use This Strategy

When you want the children to move to music

Materials Needed

Scarves or brightly colored cloth cut into long strips (crepe-paper streamers can also be used but they are less durable), music that can be quickly stopped and restarted

May I Play, Too? Asking to Join a Game or Activity

This strategy works best when it has been determined that the child is developmentally ready to participate in joint play activities. This strategy is effective with children who are high-functioning, such as children with Asperger's Syndrome.

Objective

To teach the child a strategy to use when asking to join an activity or game

When to Use This Strategy

When you want to teach the child appropriate ways to join in the activities or play of others

Materials Needed

Four index cards, glue, pictures showing: walk, stop, listen (ears with cupped hand), and "?"

What to Do

1. Glue one picture on each card. Then, lay the cards out in the following order: walk, stop, listen, and "?".

2. Tell the child that you are going to show him the steps to follow when he wants to join in a game or activity.

3. Go over each step and point to the card. For example, say, "First, you walk up to where the other children are playing." Point to the card showing " "walk." "Next, you stop and watch." Point to the card with "stop" on it. "Then, you listen," and "Last of all, you ask a question. You ask, 'May I play, too?'

4. Tell the child that you will practice each step with him. Go over each step several times, and model exactly what to do.

May I Play, Too? Asking to Join a Game or Activity

5. Ask several peers to help you demonstrate the rules for joining in a game. See if they will role-play what to do.

Helpful Hints

◆ Although this strategy is designed for children with autism, it is a good social skill for all children to learn.

◆ Ask all the children in the class to use this procedure when they want to join in a game.

◆ To encourage the child with autism to try this strategy, set up a game that you know he will especially enjoy and see if you can prompt him to request to join the game.

◆ Ask others in the class to remember that he is practicing a new skill and encourage them to let him join in, when he asks.

Time to Stop—Putting Away Toys and Activities

This strategy is most effective if you give the child ample notice that it will soon be time to clean up. Using the routine consistently will increase the likelihood that the child complies with the cleanup time.

Objective

To help the child cease playing when prompted and to put away toys without getting angry or upset

When to Use This Strategy

When you want to teach the child to help at cleanup time

Materials Needed

Small, hand-held bell or service bell

What to Do

1. Announce that it will soon be time to clean up the toys. Tell the children that when they hear the bell rung two times, it means they are to start getting ready to clean up.
2. After you ring the bell two times, wait approximately three to four minutes and ring the bell once again. Explain that this single ring means it is time to clean up.
3. Teach the class the cleanup song, sung to the tune of "Here We Go 'Round the Mulberry Bush."

This is way we clean up our toys.
Clean-up our toys, clean up our toys.
This is the way we clean up our toys.
In Miss _____'s classroom (fill in the blank with your name).

4. Tell the class that after you ring the bell once, you will start to hum the song. When they hear you humming, they must stop and finish what they are doing.
5. Sing the song and invite the class to sing along with you as they pick up the toys.
6. Go over all the steps and practice what they are to do: Two rings means a few more minutes to play, one ring means time to finish up, humming means it is time to pick up toys, and singing means it is time to pick up toys and go to _____ (whatever the next activity is).

Helpful Hints

- It may be necessary to review the steps several times before the child with autism sees this as part of the daily routine.
- Be sure to share this routine with others who may be in your classroom when you are absent.
- If the child is still playing when you get through singing, walk over to the area where he is and gently begin humming or singing the song. Pick up a toy, put it away, and ask him to help you clean up.

Once Upon a Time...Playing With Props

Once you have determined which center the child with autism seems to prefer (home-living, manipulative, science, building, and so on), select that center and plan an activity using props. For example, if the child seems to favor the science center, plan an activity with props for that center.

What to Do

1. Select the center that you want to use based on the child's preferences. Look around the center for items that can be used in pretend play.

2. Explain to a few children (no more than three), that you will tell them a story and you want them to act it out. Demonstrate and model what you want the children to do. For example, if the story is about looking for a bear, show the child how to pretend she is looking for a bear.

3. Sometimes, it is easier for the child to role-play a familiar story, such as "Goldilocks" or "The Three Little Pigs."

4. Encourage the group to make up a story and act it out.

5. A higher functioning child, such as a child with Asperger's Syndrome might be more prone to act out a scene from a movie or a familiar TV show. This is fine, as long as it is appropriate for the classroom. Sometimes, even at the preschool level, the scene may be too violent for reenacting.

6. If necessary, introduce a prop and model for the child exactly how to use it before encouraging her to begin interacting with peers.

Objective

To help the child participate in a play activity involving props

When to Use This Strategy

When you want to encourage playing with props

Materials Needed

Classroom items

Helpful Hints

◆ Experiment with different props and/or storylines to see which one works best.

◆ Later, as play becomes more advanced, encourage the children to make up their own pretend stories.

Resources Used in This Chapter

Baker, Bruce L., & A.J. Brightman. 2004. *Steps to independence: Teaching everyday skills to children with special needs (4th edition)*. Baltimore, MD: Paul H. Brookes Publishing Co.

Isbell, C. & R. Isbell. 2005. *The inclusive learning center book for preschool children with special needs*. Beltsville, MD: Gryphon House, Inc.

Kranowitz, C.S. 2003. *The out-of-sync child has fun: Safe activities for home and school—sensory-motor, appropriate, fun, and easy*. New York: The Berkley Publishing Group.

Leaf, R. & J. McEachin, (Eds.). 1999. *A work in progress*. New York: DRL Books, L.L.C.

Moor, J. 2005. *Playing, laughing, and learning with children on the autism spectrum*. London: Jessica Kingsley Publishers.

Sonders, S.A. 2003. *Giggle time: Establishing the social connection*. London: Jessica Kingsley Publishers.

Wolfberg, P. 2003. *Peer play and the autism spectrum*. Shawnee Mission, KS: Autism, Asperger Publishing Company.

Key Terms

Imaginative play: Play activities that involve using imagination.

Parallel play: Play, where one child plays near or beside another child and may even share some of the same toys, but they do not play together in a reciprocal fashion.

Peer buddy: Someone who is assigned to interact and play with a child for a given period.

Personal space: The space in which someone feels comfortable—their comfort zone.

Pretend play: Make-believe play.

Reciprocal play: Direct play with a partner where the children interact with each other.

Socialization: The ability to get along with others.

Solitary play: Playing alone or play that does not involve others.

Symbolic play: Using one object or toy to represent another, such as pretending a square block is a camera or that a cardboard box is a jet plane.

Resources | Terms

Building
Social Skills:
Getting Along With Others

Why Are Social Skills Important?

Preschool is a time when children learn the fundamental skills necessary to get along with others. It is a time when they learn how to make friends, how to treat other people, and how to interact socially. In preschool, children learn to collaborate with other children. Most children with autism have considerable difficulty behaving appropriately in social situations. In fact, one of the defining characteristics of autism is an inability to see situations from someone else's point of view.

Playing with peers

157

Children with autism don't develop social skills in the same way as their peers. While typically developing children learn social skills through observation and experience, children with autism struggle with social cues and are frequently unable to establish lasting social relationships. In order to select a social skills strategy for a child, it is important to know about the stages of social development.

What Are the Stages of Social Development?

Social development depends on many factors. For example, exposure to other children and the presence or absence of siblings in the home are contributing factors in a child's ability to interact socially. In general, social development occurs in conjunction with cognitive and emotional development. As a child matures, his social relationships will become more complex. Table 8-1 summarizes the major characteristics in the social development of children ages two to five.

Table 8-1: Major Characteristics of Social Development

Approximate Age of Child	Primary Social Characteristics
Two years old	◆ Plays alone ◆ Is egocentric and self-absorbed ◆ Depends on adults for guidance ◆ May socialize to get something, but has little understanding of the feelings and needs of others
Three years old	◆ Begins to learn to take turns ◆ Begins to know the difference between girls and boys ◆ Enjoys simple group activities ◆ Likes to help with small chores ◆ Responds to adult approval or disapproval ◆ Has a rudimentary understanding of empathy and the point of view of others
Four years old	◆ Becomes very social and plays simple games with rules ◆ Selects a peer and might even play exclusively with that peer ◆ Understands more fully that others have feelings and needs ◆ Responds when someone else is unhappy or sad
Five years old	◆ Enjoys and takes pride in accomplishments ◆ will play with friends and shows a distinct preference for specific friends ◆ Understands the abstract nature of social interactions ◆ Can usually tell the difference between a kidding remark and a remark that is serious ◆ Laughs and shows emotional responses freely

Which Social Skills Should Be Learned First?

By definition, a socially competent child has developed strong interpersonal communication skills, knows how to form relationships with peers, and understands the value of appropriately interacting with others.

Think about a child in your classroom that you would characterize as popular. Perhaps this child is always invited to birthday parties or seems to be a natural group leader. What makes this child so popular? If you observe the child, you are likely to see that she is popular because she has learned how to make other children feel important, to recognize the preferences of others, and to behave in socially acceptable ways. In other words, she has learned what it takes to be liked by others. Learning how to adapt to a social situation and behaving accordingly is a skill she will use throughout her life. Therefore, an important characteristic of the socially competent child is that she knows how to make adaptations to her own behavior so that others will want to be her friend.

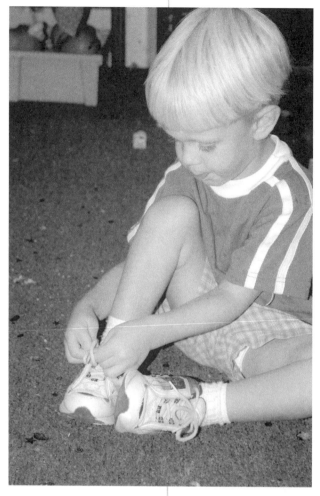

Socially competent preschoolers take pride in their accomplishments.

Another characteristic of the socially competent preschooler is that he is able to control his own behavior. Studies have consistently shown that children are more likely to want to play with a child whom they perceive as having self-control. Generally, self-controlled children manage their anger and do not have violent outbursts. In addition, they are not aggressive toward themselves or others.

Finally, socially competent preschoolers have self-confidence. As a result, they are not afraid to try new things or experiment with novel situations. Confident children enjoy things that challenge them and feel a sense of accomplishment when they succeed at a new task. When a peer doesn't want to play with him, a confident child either adjusts his behavior so the peer will play with him, or he finds someone else who will. All the characteristics of a socially competent child depend on his being able to use and understand language.

Other children help social development.

All the characteristics of a socially competent child depend on his being able to use and understand language.

With this in mind, consider a child with autism who does not know how to interact and read social cues, cannot control his behavior, and lacks the confidence to enjoy novel situations. Further, the child probably has no idea how to interpret, much less understand, the preferences and feelings of others, and more than likely has a significant language delay. For these reasons, social skills training for children with autism is critically important.

How Do I Teach Social Skills to a Child With Autism?

Most children learn social skills through experience and observation. They watch how other children act and what other children do in social settings. Then, based on their observations, they imitate the behavior of others. For children with autism, it is not as easy as that. They often lack the ability to learn social skills through observation or to interpret social cues. While typically-developing children are likely to benefit from observing a social situation, a child with autism usually needs more. He must learn techniques that will help him respond appropriately in social settings. One technique that helps children with autism learn social skills is called the social story.

What Are Social Stories?

Social stories present appropriate social behaviors in the context of a story. Author Carol Gray developed this concept. Each story includes answers to questions that children with autism need to know in order to interact with others. In other words, a social story answers who, what, when, where, and why questions about social interaction. In some senses, a social story can teach the child with autism to respond to others, even if he does not fully understand why he is doing so. By simply imitating in a real-life setting what happened in the story, the child begins to experience some semblance of social interaction with a peer.

Developing social skills through play

Social stories help the child with autism learn to predict how others might act in a social situation, by giving her a better understanding of the thoughts, feelings, and points of view of other children. Social stories also help the child with autism learn more about what might be expected of her in such a setting. However, before deciding how to use social stories, it is important to observe the child and decide which of the three types of social impairment best applies.

What Are the Three Types of Social Impairment?

The first type of social impairment is characterized by the socially avoidant child. This child may try to escape a social situation by having a tantrum, being aggressive toward others, or hiding in a closet. Some children are socially avoidant because the environment has become too much for them—the noise, smells, lights, and overwhelming number of other children is more than they can stand. The only way they know how to react is to escape the situation altogether.

The second type of social impairment includes children who are socially indifferent. Although they may not avoid socialization by withdrawing or getting upset, they do not actively attempt to interact with others. Children in this category are happier being alone and have considerable difficulty making and keeping friends. A socially indifferent child allows social interactions to go on around him while remaining passive and makes no attempt to join in the interaction.

Social awkwardness is the defining characteristic of the final type of social impairment. These children tend to be higher-functioning. For example, many

Turning away from play

children with Asperger's syndrome fit into this category. While they will interact socially, their conversations seem to be centered on subjects of interest to them. They may talk about something they like but fail to respond when another child wants to change the subject or offer a comment. Socially awkward children do not understand the rules of polite conversation and can't grasp the concept of small talk. The general rule for children in this category is, "If it's not about something that interests me—it's not worth talking about." Socially awkward children probably benefit the most from the use of social stories.

How Do I Write a Social Story?

Once you have determined in which category of social impairment a child belongs, it is time to begin observing the child. General guidelines for observing the child include:

◆ Observe the child on multiple occasions.
◆ Watch the child in a variety of settings.
◆ Make careful notes about his interests and preferences.
◆ Make a list of the children he plays with most often.
◆ Determine if there are certain activities, toys, or people that upset him.

Before writing a social story, it is always a good idea to call a team meeting. Bring together the people who work with the child and ask them to comment on how they have observed him in social situations. Compare their observations with yours. Next, decide on what social skill you want to work on first. Remember, children with autism often have social difficulties because they cannot seem to understand what is expected of them. Let's look at some examples.

William, a child with Asperger's syndrome, likes baseball. He frequently puts on his baseball glove, gets his ball, and approaches a peer. William does not understand that the peer may be engaged in doing something else. Instead of asking the peer to play ball with him, William throws the ball at the other child. When the peer turns away from William, he gets upset.

An appropriate social story for William might include how to ask others to play with him.

Amanda, a child with autism, frequently screams when she wants to go to the computer center. Once, upon entering, she found other children working collaboratively on the computer. Instead of asking if she might join in, she attempted to push another child out of the chair.

Amanda would benefit from a social story that involves learning to ask others to let her have a turn or learning how to ask if she can join in a collaborative activity.

Once you have determined which social skill you want to focus on, it is time to start writing a social story. As you begin to write, keep in mind that social stories are:

- short,
- written in first person,
- usually in present tense, and
- designed to help the child learn how to act in a social situation.

Four types of sentences make up a social story: descriptive, perspective, directive, and control. Descriptive sentences address who, what, where, and why of the social situation. Perspective sentences give information about the thoughts, feelings, and emotions of others. Directive sentences tell the child how he might respond to the situation. In other words, a directive sentence suggests a specific action on the part of the child that will enhance the social interaction.

Control sentences are more complex and are usually only used with high-functioning children. The control sentence is something that serves as a cue or hint to remind the child how to react in a social setting. Control sentences are generally not appropriate for preschool children. When they are used with younger children, they must be short and easy to remember. For example, after learning about conversation, the child might remember to stop, look, and listen: stop after he has spoken, look at the other person, and listen to what the other person is saying.

According to Carol Gray, author and developer of "social stories," a tool to teach social skills to children with autism, it is important that for each directive sentence, a ratio of at least three descriptive or perspective sentences be used. Later, as the child becomes more socially competent, stories can be written with no directive sentences. The child can learn to decide for himself how he should respond or react. Gray also recommends that absolute statements be replaced with statements that are more flexible. For example, instead of writing, "I will ask for a turn" or "I can sit in a circle," the child might say, "I will try to ask for a turn" or "I will try to sit in a circle."

Remember, children with autism often have social difficulties because they cannot seem to understand what is expected of them.

Let's look at a social story written for William, the child who enjoys baseball. Remember, his problem is that he does not know how to ask other children to play catch with him.

I like to play baseball. I have a new ball and glove. I want Tom to play catch with me. Sometimes, Tom is having fun playing with his cars. When I want Tom to play with me, I will tap him on the shoulder. I will say, "Tom, would you play ball with me?" I will try not to just throw the ball at Tom when I want him to play with me. I will try to learn to ask Tom to play ball.

Finally, let's look at a social story written for Amanda, who wants to join Lauren in an art activity but does not know how to ask.

I go to the art center. Other children are playing there. Lauren is painting at the easel. I want to paint, too! I will try to wait until Lauren is finished. I will try to ask if I can paint at the easel with Lauren. If she says no, I will go to another center.

Hi! My Name Is _____.

This strategy is most effective when the child is relaxed and not anxious.

Strategy

What to Do

1. Teach the child the process involved in meeting someone new:

   ◆ Walk up to the person you want to meet.
   ◆ Stand one arm-length away. (**Note:** Practice where to stand, as children with autism often have difficulty knowing how close or how far back to stand.)
   ◆ Look at the person's face. Smile.
   ◆ Say, "Hi, my name is _____ (fill in the child's name)."
   ◆ Wait!
   ◆ Say, "I like to _____ (fill in something the child likes to do)."
   ◆ Wait!
   ◆ Say, "Bye."
   ◆ Wait! Walk away.

2. Go through each step, one at a time. Ask the child to do each step immediately after you model it for her.
3. Provide opportunities for the child to practice. Ask other classmates if they would like to pretend they are meeting someone new.
4. Review the steps often.
5. At first, the child may not be able to remember all the steps. If she forgets, remind her gently by saying, "Next, you _____."

Helpful Hints

◆ After the child has practiced several times in the classroom, take her to another part of the school and introduce her to someone she has not met.
◆ As often as possible, remind the class how to introduce themselves to someone new.

Objective

To teach the child to introduce himself and say "Hello" and "Goodbye" to a new person

When to Use This Strategy

When you are teaching the child to meet someone new

Materials Needed

None

Something Good About Me!

This strategy works best when the child is verbal or after the child has started using either signs or picture cards to communicate consistently.

Objective

To teach the child to say something that he likes about himself

When to Use This Strategy

When you want to help the child build self-esteem and identify his strengths

Materials Needed

None

What to Do

1. Teach the class the following song.

    ME (sung to the tune of "Mary Had a Little Lamb")
    I am very proud of me,
    Proud of me, proud of me
    I am very proud of me
    Because I can _____ (fill in the blank)!

2. The first time you sing the song, fill in the blank yourself and add motions. For example:

    I am very proud of me,
    Proud of me, proud of me.
    I am very proud of me
    Because I can hop! (Hop one time)

3. Sing the song several times, adding new verses each time.

4. After the children have sung the song several times, ask each child to tell you one thing they are proud of about themselves. After the child has said what he is proud of about himself, sing the song a different way. For example, if John says he is proud of himself because he can throw a ball, you would sing:

    We are very proud of John,
    Proud of John, proud of John.
    We are very proud of John
    Because he can throw a ball!

5. Repeat the activity with each child in the group, until everyone has had a turn. If the child with autism cannot think of anything to say, you may have

Something Good About Me!

Taking turns is important.

to make a suggestion or ask his peers to help.

6. Try this song when a child is just learning a new skill as well. For example:

I am very proud of Nakisha,
Proud of Nakisha, proud of Nakisha.
I am very proud of Nakisha
Because she is learning to share!

Helpful Hints

◆ Later, after the children have learned how to play the game and sing the song, see if they will play the game by saying something they are proud of about someone else.

◆ Share the song with the child's family so they can sing it, too.

Talk to Me!

Learning when and how to initiate an interaction is often very difficult for children with autism. This strategy works best when the child is verbal or using signs or communication cards.

Objective

To help the child learn how to have a conversation with others

When to Use This Strategy

When you want to help a child learn how to stop, look, and listen when others are talking

Materials Needed

None

What to Do

1. Write a simple social story for a conversation. It might go something like this:

   I *want to talk to* _____ (fill in a child's name).
   I *will walk up to* _____ (fill in a child's name).
   I *will say,* "Hi!"
   I *will wait for him to say,* "Hi."
   I *will look at him and say,* "What are you doing?"
   I *will wait for him to talk.*
   I *will say,* "That sounds like fun."
   I *will wait for him to talk.*
   I *will look at him.*
   I *will say,* "Bye!"

2. Ask the child with autism to say the name of or point to someone he would like to talk with. If he does not do so, then you point to someone and say, "Let's talk to _____ (fill in the peer's name)."

3. Go over these steps with the child. Ask him to imitate each step as you read the social story. Review the steps often.

4. Ask a peer to help you practice this routine with the child.

5. Go through each step often. If the child does not wait or starts to walk away, remind him what to do next.

6. If the child is non-verbal, adapt the sequence using picture cards.

Helpful Hints

- Post cue cards in the classroom that show the steps in a conversation.
- Role play with small groups of children.

Strategy

Telephone Talk: Following Simple Directions

This strategy is designed to be used with a child and another adult or a child and a peer. This strategy is not designed for a large group. This strategy can be used with a child who is nonverbal as well as a child who is verbal. It works best when the child is not upset or not already involved in another activity.

What to Do

1. Using the scissors, make a small hole in the bottom of each cup (adult-only step). Put a piece of string or yarn through each hole and tie a large knot.

2. Tell the child with autism you are going to play a game with him. Place one cup to your ear and hold it there. Ask the child to take the other cup.

3. If the child is hesitant, ask a peer to help you demonstrate what to do.

4. Say something to the person on the other end of the phone, such as, "Touch your nose."

5. Continue to tell the person to do something simple, such as, "Wave at me" or "Turn around once."

6. Remember that preschool children are normally quite curious, so others may want to play, too.

7. After you have given a few simple directions, see if the child on the other end of the line will give you a command.

Objective

To teach the child to follow a simple direction while interacting with a peer or an adult

When to Use This Strategy

When the child is ready to learn to follow simple directions

Materials Needed

Two Styrofoam cups, string or yarn, adult scissors

Helpful Hints

◆ Tell the children that this is like a real phone in that one person receives a message and other person responds.

◆ After the child is more familiar with the game, try to get him to play it with his peers.

◆ As the child learns to follow one-step directions, add more information, such as two-step directions. For example, "Touch your nose and then wave at me."

What to Do? What to Do? (A Poem for Solving a Simple Problem)

This strategy can be used in both large and small groups. The child will benefit most from this strategy after she has been in your class for a few weeks and you have modeled simple problem-solving skills, such as sharing, speaking softly, waiting for others to have a turn, and learning to handle a change in routine.

Objective

To find different ways to solve a problem

When to Use This Strategy

When you want to model ways to solve everyday problems

Materials Needed

Chart paper or poster board and pictures to decorate the poster, if desired

What to Do

1. Copy the following poem on a piece of chart paper or poster board:

   What to Do? What to Do? by Clarissa Willis

   I go to school almost every day.
   Sometimes things get in my way.
   I get mad and want to fight.

   But I know that is not right.
   So, I need some help from you.
   Can you tell me what to do?

2. Read the poem with the group. Then, go back and read one line and see if they will say the line after you. Go through this several times, before going on to the next step.

3. After you have read the poem together several times. Tell the group that this time you will tell them about a pretend situation, and see if someone can help solve it. Ask the children to raise their hands, if they know how to solve the problem.

4. Read, then say the poem together. After the last line, give the group a simple problem to solve. For example:

   Two children both want to play with the same toy. Your favorite center (or activity) is already full and you must go somewhere else. You want to join in a game others are playing. You want to ask someone to share with you.

5. Even if the child with autism does not participate, chances are she is listening to the activity and might, in time, start to raise her hand. If she does not, try calling on her by name such as, "Roberta, what would you do?"

6. As the year progresses and children become better problem-solvers, try to make the problems more difficult or more specific, such as "Yesterday, I noticed you watched as Lawrence and Bart played. How might you have asked to join in?" or "Tomorrow, Officer Davis is going to talk to us about his job as a police officer. How will you act when he comes to visit our class?"

Helpful Hints

- This activity can be especially useful in helping children with autism generalize that a problem may be different but the strategy for solving it is the same.
- Use the poem as a distracter if a child starts to get upset.

Learning to Say, "Thank You"

This strategy should be taught one-on-one. To use this strategy, the child must be able to say or sign, "Thank you."

What to Do

1. Determine if you are going to encourage the child to say, "Thank you" or sign "Thank you." (You may decide to do both.)

2. If you are going to use the sign, demonstrate how to use it. The sign for "thank you" is made by touching your lips with the tips of the fingers of your right hand. Move your hand away from your face, palms upward. Smile. If you use two hands with this sign, it means, "Thank you very much."

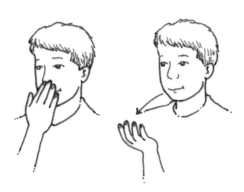

3. Tell the child that you are going to teach him what to do when someone does something for him. Explain that saying or signing "thank you" lets the other person know that you like what he did for you.

4. Recite the following jingle for the child:

   When you like what others do
   Smile at them (smile) *and say, "Thank you!"*

5. Use the poem frequently with all of the children in the class.

6. Model saying and/or using the sign for "thank you" when anyone in the class does something for someone else.

Helpful Hints

◆ Send a letter home telling the child's parents that you are working on saying, "Thank you!" (Include a copy of the jingle for them to use at home.)

◆ Praise children when they say or sign, "Thank you."

Objective

To help the child learn to say or sign, "Thank you" when someone does something for him

When to Use This Strategy

When the child has learned or is beginning to learn to communicate his wants/needs to others

Materials Needed

None

Help Wanted! Peer Buddy

This strategy works best when you have observed children in the classroom and determined who might have the skills and patience to be a peer buddy.

Objective

To use the following guidelines when selecting peer buddies and demonstrating how to be a peer buddy for a child with autism

When to Use This Strategy

When you have determined that the child has developed adequate social skills to benefit from interaction with a peer buddy

Materials Needed

Three large index cards, markers

What to Do

1. Write one word on each index card: "stay," "play," and "talk."

2. Carefully select a candidate for a peer buddy. Consider the child's maturity and communication skills. Also, think about selecting a peer buddy who has some of the same interests as the child with autism.

3. Talk to the peer-buddy candidate and ask her if she would like to help you for a few minutes. Say that you want her to help you _____ (be very specific). For example, "Tamika, I would like for you to help me teach Roberto how to play." Watch her to see if she shows any signs of being resistant to the idea.

4. Say, "I need your help today during the first five minutes of free activity time. I am going to teach you just what to do. First (hold up the card that has "stay" written on it), I want you to stay with Roberto for a few minutes."

5. Pause, and try to determine if the child understood what you want her to do. Say. "Next (hold up the card that has "play" written on it), I want you to play with Roberto." And, "Last, I want you to talk (hold up the card that has "talk" written on it) to Roberto, even if he does not talk to you."

6. Ask the child for an answer. "Will you help me?"

7. Reinforce the child's answer, "Thank you. I knew I could count on you. Let's review the three things I want you to do." Review the three steps: stay, play, talk.

8. Say, "Remember, you just have to do this during the first part of free activity time. When I want you to help me, I will come and tap you on the shoulder." Smile, nod, and thank the child again for helping you.

Helpful Hints

◆ Keep in mind that relationships take time.

◆ If the child says, "No" when you ask her to be a peer buddy, don't try to convince her otherwise—find another child instead.

◆ The most outgoing children are often not the best peer buddies, as they tend to be demanding.

◆ Look for a child who seems to be a natural helper or one who seems to have an ability to be tolerant of others.

◆ Avoid assigning permanent peer buddies. If a relationship develops between two children, that is great. However, keep in mind that the main objective is to find a buddy to be with the child for a specified amount of time.

Three Breaths Away (a Strategy for Calming Down)

Deep breathing is a technique that also works well with other children. Teach it to the entire class.

What to Do

1. Tell the child you are going to show him something he can do when he is getting stressed by people or situations.
2. Tell him that it involves breathing. First say, "I want you to breathe with me. We will take a big breath, hold it, and then see if we can blow all the breath out."
3. Practice together. Take a deep breath. Hold. Blow out all the air.
4. Next say, "I will bring my hands together (place your hands in front of you like you are going to clap)."
5. Then say, "Now, I will put my hands down and take another breath."
6. Repeat this process, until you have done it three times.
7. Say to the child, "Next time you think you are getting upset, come and get me and we will breathe."
8. Try to provide opportunities for the child to practice this technique.
9. Remember, if the child can focus on breathing before he gets too upset, the strategy has a much better chance of being successful.

Helpful Hints

♦ It may take several times before the child understands what you are asking him to do.

♦ Don't give up—keep trying. Once the child learns to do this strategy, it can greatly reduce outbursts.

♦ Share the strategy with the child's parents and encourage them to practice it, too.

Objective

To learn a simple technique to help the child with autism calm himself so he won't get upset with others

When to Use This Strategy

When you need to give the child with autism an alternative to getting mad or becoming aggressive

Materials Needed

None

Building a Sense of Community With a Job

This strategy works best when you have had time to observe the child and match him with a classroom job that suits his needs and interests.

Objective

To assign the child with autism a specific classroom task

When to Use This Strategy

When you wish to build a sense of community and make the child feel part of the classroom

Materials Needed

A picture of each child placed on the bulletin board with space under it to attach an object that represents the child's job for the week or month; pictures to represent each classroom task, such as a cloth, a block, a piece of paper wadded up, a sign that says "caboose," a book, a mat for use in group time, a napkin

What to Do

1. Hold up objects that represent the classroom jobs. Tell the children that the jobs will change in _____ weeks or days, so that they know they will have the opportunity to change jobs. (If you prefer, have a picture that shows the job so the child can attach the picture to the space under his picture.)

2. Tell the children that if they are interested in that job they should raise their hands.

3. If more than one child volunteers and it is a job that two children can do, such as cleaning up the block area or handing out napkins for snack time, then let the children share the job.

4. Explain that one job will be the line leader for the week and one job will be the caboose (last person in line). Tell the group that the leader is important because she will be first in line, and the caboose is also important because he is the one who must make sure all the other children are in line.

5. You may be surprised to find that the child with autism will raise his hand to volunteer for a job. If he does not, then you could assign him a job by saying, "Thomas, you will be the napkin delivery person this week. That means you will give everyone a napkin during snack time."

6. If necessary, assign another child to help the child with autism.

7. After you fill each job, ask the child to go and attach the object that represents the job under their picture.

8. After each child has been assigned a task, model for the child with autism exactly what he is to do in his job. Break each step down and teach him one step at a time.

9. The first time the child performs his job, it may be necessary to act as a job coach and assist him.

Helpful Hints

◆ If a child cannot do a complete job independently, let him participate partially. For example, if his job is to hand out napkins at snack time and he cannot do it, perhaps he can walk beside a peer and hold the napkins while the peer passes them out.

◆ Use the whole concept of jobs to demonstrate good behavior on a job such as, saying or signing, "Thank you."

◆ Because resistance to a change in routine is very common in children with autism, you may want to change his job less often than you do the other children. While you do not want a child to keep a job all year, keeping it several months may be helpful to both you and the child with autism.

◆ The more a child does something, the more confident he will become and the more he will enjoy being successful at the task.

The Itsy Bitsy Spider! (Learning to Try Again!)

This is also a super ego booster for the child's family when they see the child is trying to learn something.

Objective

To encourage the child with autism to try something again if she has failed in the past

When to Use This Strategy

When you want to build self-esteem and give the child the message that you want her to keep trying

Materials Needed

Cutouts of cute spiders (use craft foam, card stock, or felt), magnetic tape

What to Do

1. Make refrigerator magnets. Attach a small strip of magnetic tape to each cutout spider. On each spider, write, "I got the Itsy Bitsy Spider Award today for _____ (fill in the blank with what the child tried to do)."

2. Sing the song, "The Itsy Bitsy Spider" with the children. Do the hand motions, too.

3. Ask the children if they know what the song is about. Talk about how the spider tried again and again to go up the spout.

4. Tell the children it does not matter if the spider ever made it up the spout. What is important is that he tried.

5. them if they think it was hard for the spider to climb up the spout. Ask them to tell you something that is hard for them to do.

6. Hold up one of the Itsy Bitsy Spider cutouts. Read what it says. Tell the children that you are going to be watching them, and if you see someone who keeps trying, you are going to give that person an Itsy Bitsy Spider Award.

7. Talk about how important it is to keep trying and not to give up. Sing the song again.

Use books that teach a lesson.

The Itsy Bitsy Spider! (Learning to Try Again!)

8. Place the Itsy Bitsy Spider Award magnet in the child's take-home folder with a note to his family. Encourage them to place the magnet on the refrigerator at home and to praise the child for his effort at trying something new.

I won the Itsy Bitsy Spider Award

Helpful Hints

◆ When you see the child try something that is hard, be sure to praise him.

◆ Remind the child that the spider never gave up.

◆ When the child gets an Itsy Bitsy Spider to wear, write down what he did on the spider and in your notes. (It will help you when it is conference time to point out that the child continues to try.)

Resources Used in This Chapter

Abrams, P. & L. Henriques. 2004. *The autistic spectrum: Parent's daily helper.* Berkeley, CA: Ulysses Press.

Baker, J.E. 2001. *The social skills picture book: Teaching play, emotion and communication to children with autism.* Arlington, TX: Future Horizons, Inc.

McCabe, P. & P. Meller. 2004. *The relationship between language and social competence: How language impairment affects social growth.* Psychology in the Schools, 41(3), 313-322.

Sigman, M. & L. Capps. 1997. *Children with autism: A developmental perspective.* Cambridge: Harvard University Press.

Wallin, J.M. 2005. *Social stories: An introduction to social stories.* Retrieved August 5, 2005, from http://www.polyxo.com/social stories/introduction.html

Williams, D. 1996. *Autism: An inside-out approach: An innovative look at the mechanics of autism and its developmental cousins.* London: Jessica Kingsley Publishers.

Wolfberg, P. 2003. *Peer play and the autism spectrum: The art of guiding children's socialization and imagination.* Shawnee Mission, KS: Autism Asperger Publishing Company.

Key Terms

Control sentence: Control sentences are used in social stories and serve as a cue or hint to remind the child how to react in a social setting.

Descriptive sentence: Type of sentence used in social stories to address the who, what, where, and why of the social situation.

Directive sentence: Type of sentence used in social stories to tell the child how to respond to a situation. It suggests a specific action on the part of the child that will enhance the social interaction.

Egocentric: Self-absorbed, believing the world revolves around them.

Perspective sentence: Type of sentence used in social stories to provide information about the thoughts, feelings, and emotions of others.

Social story: A strategy designed by Carol Gray where stories are used to help children with autism learn social interaction skills in the context of a story.

Socially avoidant: A type of social impairment characterized by a child who tries to escape social situations.

Socially awkward: A type of social impairment characterized by a child who does not understand the give-and-take nature of a social interaction.

Socially competent: By definition, a socially competent child has developed strong interpersonal communication skills, knows how to form relationships with peers, and understands the value of appropriately interacting with others.

Socially indifferent: A type of social impairment characterized by a child who is indifferent to social situations.

Lights!
Camera!
Action!
Sensory Integration and Autism

What Exactly Is Sensory Integration?

Sensory Integration (SI) is a process that occurs in the brain. It allows us to take in information through our senses, organize it, and respond accordingly to the environment. It is also the process that allows us to filter out any unneeded sensory information. For example, when you walk into a noisy cafeteria, it is sensory integration that gives you the ability to filter out the surrounding noise so that you can enjoy your lunch or chat with a friend. When asked to name their senses, most

Select activities that encourage the child to use his motor skills.

people think only of the obvious ones: sight, hearing, touch, taste, and smell. Nevertheless, there are two "hidden" senses that are just as important.

What Are the Hidden Senses?

The hidden senses include the vestibular sense and the proprioceptive sense. Both of these senses play an important role in helping the child integrate all the information he receives from the environment.

The vestibular sense provides information through the inner ear about balance, movement, and gravity. In other words, it is the vestibular sense that lets a child know how to position his head and body in relation to the earth.

The vestibular sense affects:
◆ the sense of balance or equilibrium,
◆ the way the eyes and hands work together (eye-hand coordination),
◆ the ability to move both sides of the body together, and
◆ movement of the head.

Using touch is important.

The proprioceptive system receives information from joints, muscles, and ligaments. It is this sense that lets a child know where his body parts are and what they are doing. For example, information provided for a child by this system might tell her how far it is for her to reach to pick up a toy and how much pressure is comfortable or uncomfortable to parts of her body.

These two senses work together to help regulate the nervous system and build the foundation for purposeful movement. When a child cannot regulate the information he receives from his senses, he is often diagnosed with a Sensory Integration Disorder.

What Do You Mean by a Sensory Integration Disorder?

Almost 50 years ago, an occupational therapist named Jean Ayres described a condition that resulted from an insufficient process in the brain. She used the term Sensory Integration Dysfunction (SI

Dysfunction) to describe a child who is unable to analyze and respond appropriately to the information he receives from his senses. A child with Sensory Integration Dysfunction has problems adapting to the everyday sensations that others take for granted. Today, the terms Sensory Integration Dysfunction, Sensory Integration Disorder, and Sensory Modulation Disorder are used interchangeably. Regardless of which term is used, many experts believe that a sensory integration problem is the root cause of many of the behaviors commonly seen in children with autism.

Do You Mean That Children With Autism See or Hear Differently?

Children with autism can hear and see just like other children. What many are unable to do, however, is to take the information that they see, hear, taste, feel, or touch and translate it into a meaningful response. In other words, what may seem like normal classroom lighting to you might seem like megawatt spotlights to the child with autism. The normal chatter heard in a classroom where children work and play in centers can be unbearably loud to a child with sensory integration issues. Children with autism are often unable to regulate or modulate the input they receive through their senses. Because such information is sometimes so overpowering, they will have problems learning and interacting in their environments.

Remember, most children enjoy activities that involve movement, such as dancing to a favorite tune or jumping up and down. In addition, preschool children thrive on opportunities to touch new things and enjoy using their hands for such activities as making a mountain from clay or painting with their fingers. Preschool children can sit on a carpet square and listen to a story, play in the dirt or sandbox, and smell a fresh flower with delight. However, for a child with autism who has a sensory integration disorder, these activities can be frightening, confusing, and overwhelming.

How Will I Know If a Child Has a Sensory Integration Disorder?

You will know it by observation, through information you receive from others, and by educating yourself about ways to recognize it. A few of the most common red flags that a child has a sensory integration disorder include unusual responses to touch, adverse responses to moving and being moved, a lack of tolerance for noise and light, and an unwillingness to taste or try new foods.

What may seem like normal classroom lighting to you might seem like megawatt spotlights to the child with autism.

Movement activities are fun sensory experiences.

The following are a few examples of how a child with sensory integration disorder might respond to everyday classroom situations:

Scott walks into your room and looks around. He immediately goes to the sink in the back of the room and turns on the faucet. He watches as the water comes out. He places his hands in the water. He fails to notice anything except the running water. In fact, he probably still has his backpack and coat on as he feels the water.

It is time to get ready for lunch and you have called Maria, by name, several times. Instead of responding, she continues to stare at the rotating blades of the ceiling fan as they whirl around. A few minutes earlier, when a classmate was sharpening a pencil, Maria responded by looking around frantically. Yet now she does not seem to hear you call her name.

Hal arrives in your classroom and you start to say, "Good morning." Instead of speaking or looking at you, he begins to tell you that the bookshelf in the corner has been moved since yesterday. He can talk about nothing but his concern over the bookcase being out of place.

Mi-Ling does not enjoy circle time. She will not sit still while you read. She stands up and begins to spin around and around in front of her chair.

These are all examples of how a child with autism who has a sensory integration disorder might respond. Rather than being over-sensitive (hypersensitive) to sensory stimulation, as are the children in the examples above, some children with autism are actually under-sensitive (hyposensitive). They seem to be in another sphere where they can't see, hear, feel, or touch anything at all. Children who are under-sensitive to sensory information are at great risk for getting hurt. Because they don't often respond to sound, they may walk in front of a car. A child who is under-sensitive might pick up a hot object or fall down a flight of stairs without ever making a sound.

How Do I Know If a Child Is Over-Sensitive or Under-Sensitive?

Table 9-1 serves as a guide to the degree of response a child might have with respect to the senses. However, the child's occupational therapist is your best resource for information about sensory integration disorder.

Table 9-1: Sense Responses

Sense	Over-Sensitive	Under-Sensitive
Vision (sight)	◆ Covers his eyes when the lights are too bright ◆ Overwhelmed by too many colors and items in the classroom ◆ Rubs his eyes or squints his eyes frequently	◆ Does not respond to light ◆ Holds items close to her face as if she can't see them ◆ Stares at flickering fluorescent lights
Sound	◆ Covers his ears ◆ Responds to sounds other children ignore ◆ Will act as if he can't hear when you call his name, but then responds when a child drops a toy ◆ Yells with fingers in ears	◆ Speaks loudly ◆ Turns the volume up on the TV or computer ◆ Sings loudly ◆ Always plays with toys that make loud noises
Smell	◆ Holds her nose at common odors ◆ Sniffs the air or sniffs other people	◆ Ignores bad odors ◆ May sniff people or toys
Touch (Tactile)	◆ Gets upset when someone touches him ◆ Very sensitive to textures and materials ◆ Opposed to getting dirty or touching certain toys ◆ Scratches at his skin or startles when something touches him	◆ Bumps into people ◆ Chews on items frequently ◆ Unaware of temperature changes ◆ Seemingly unable to tell when he is in pain or hurt ◆ Does not cry when he falls down
Taste	◆ Gags when she eats ◆ Only eats food of a certain texture ◆ Sensitive to hot or cold foods	◆ Wants only spicy food ◆ Adds lots of pepper or salt to her food ◆ Licks objects or toys
Movement	◆ Does not like to move, dance, climb, or hop ◆ Sways ◆ Seems to walk "off-balance"	◆ Does not get dizzy when he whirls or turns around ◆ Loves to move fast ◆ In constant motion ◆ Rocks back and forth ◆ Moves his body all the time

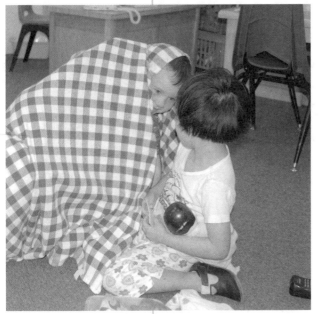

Getting under a blanket is a sensory game.

Children with sensory integration disorders sometimes respond well to items that enable them to calm down so that they can better organize all the input they receive through their senses.

What Can I Do to Help a Child With Sensory Integration Disorder?

Children with sensory integration disorders sometimes respond well to items that enable them to calm down so that they can better organize all the input they receive through their senses. Some examples of such calming objects (calmers) and organizers include: things to chew on (chewies), toys that vibrate, weighted vests, soft things that they can squeeze, beanbag chairs or therapy balls to sit on, and stretchy material such as latex that they can use to make a body cocoon.

The most common calmers and organizers include:

Chewies: For a child with issues relating to touch, chewing on something soft can be very relaxing. Chewies can be purchased from companies that specialize in sensory integration materials.

Vibrating toys: Vibration can be very calming to the proprioceptive system. Examples of vibrating items might include pens, toothbrushes, toys, pillows, and cell phones.

Weighted objects: A weighted object might be used to help a child who has difficulty with balance or with his proprioceptive system. A weighted vest, back pack, fanny pack, or blanket can help the child feel more grounded and less concerned about his sense of movement. Deep pressure helps children calm down.

Oral motor activities: Designed to help the child with issues related to his mouth and to touch. Blowing bubbles, eating crunchy foods, biting on a washcloth and blowing a cotton ball across the table with a straw can help the child satisfy her need for oral stimulation and movement.

What Can I Do to Make Sure That a Child With Autism Does Not Go Into Sensory Overload?

One of the most important things you can do is to make sure that the light in the classroom is not too bright. Florescent lights can be especially distracting for children with autism. Look for ways you can use indirect lighting (lamps, for example), or at the very least, non-florescent overhead lights.

Regulate the noise so that it is not so loud that a child is unable to function. Watch for signs that the child is being overwhelmed by the noise in the classroom; for example, if he begins to look around the room nervously, begins fidgeting, or covers his ears with his hands. Provide a quiet place for the child to go to desensitize and get away from the noise.

Activity with pressure and space

There are, of course, times when noise is unavoidable. For example, when the teacher says it is time to go outside, the children in the class put away their toys. This is can be a noisy few minutes. Paul begins to scream, because the noise resulting from everyone rushing around to put things in bins, on shelves, and in containers is just too loud for him. To alleviate the problem, his teacher asks her assistant to take Paul to the restroom while the class puts away the toys. The trip to the restroom serves two important purposes: first, it alleviates Paul's screaming because he is no longer experiencing the loud classroom; and second, it gives Paul a predictable bathroom schedule. Paul is happier and so is his teacher.

AVOID SENSORY OVERLOAD

- Use indirect lighting or non-florescent overhead lighting.
- Regulate the noise level in the classroom.
- Use textures to calm children.
- Use mild, natural scents in the classroom.

Consider the texture of the materials in your learning centers, and place items with textures that you know the child might enjoy. If experience has shown that he seems to do better with soft textures, provide a softer surface for him to play on, such as a mat or craft foam. Using something as simple as a foam hair curler as a pencil grip can make all the difference in whether a child learns to write or avoids it all together. A child who can never sit on a carpet square during circle time might be more content sitting on a beanbag chair or balancing himself on a large therapy ball.

Be aware of the smells in your classroom. To you, the sweet smell of rose scented air fresher might be pleasing and enhance your classroom. However, it could interfere with the ability of a child with autism to learn. If you use scents in the classroom, use natural ones, and then only after you have determined that the child with autism can tolerate them. For example, try peppermint, lavender, or vanilla, instead of sweet flowery scents.

Strategy

Weighted Vest

The weight from the vest will enable the child to feel more comfortable while he is working, and, as a result, he will be able to focus more attentively on the activity.

Objective

To construct a weighted vest for a child with issues related to the proprioceptive system

When to Use This Strategy

When you want the child to help a child focus on an activity

Materials Needed

Smock with pockets, large shirt with sleeves cut off, or child's vest; cloth for additional pockets; small cloth bags; salt, sand, or uncooked rice; needle and thread; Velcro (the kind that is sewed in place)

What to Do

1. Use a smock with pockets or a large shirt with the sleeves cut off. A vest with pockets may also work.

2. Add two more pockets to the back of the shirt or smock. Place the back pockets approximately the same place on the vest where the front pockets are located. The result is a vest with four pockets, two in the front and two in the back.

3. Make the weights by filling small cloth bags with salt, sand, or rice. Sew the bags shut. Each bag should weigh no more than 4 ounces. Place weights in vest pockets and Velcro the pockets shut.

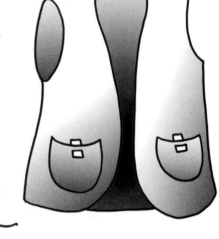

Helpful Hints

♦   Experiment with various amounts of filler. Try some that are a little heavier and some that are lighter in weight.

♦   Provide fabric markers and encourage child to decorate the vest with his artwork.

♦   One variation is to make a weighted neck wrap. Add eyes and a cloth mouth and the child has a funny snake to wear around his neck.

♦   Yard sales, flea markets, and thrift stores are good places to find old vests.

Snuggle Blanket

A snuggle blanket is designed for a child with tactile sensitivity and issues with her proprioceptive system.

What to Do

1. Purchase three to four yards of Lycra or Spandex material.
2. Select a color and pattern that you know the child will enjoy.
3. Sew a small ½" to 1" hem around the material to keep it from fraying.
4. Hang the blanket in a location that is convenient to the child. She can retrieve the blanket and wrap up in it for comfort whenever she feels overwhelmed.

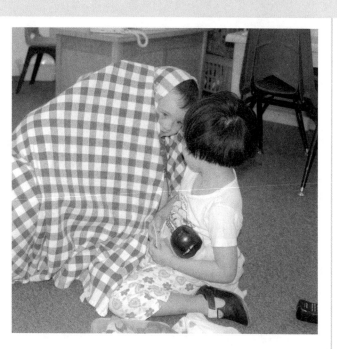

Helpful Hints

◆ Traditionally, Lycra or Spandex works best. However, you might experiment with other types of fabric.
◆ Make several blankets and encourage other children to use them as well.

Objective

To make a blanket that the child can wrap herself in as a way for her to calm down when things are becoming overwhelming

When to Use This Strategy

When a child is feeling too overwhelmed by the environment

Materials Needed

Three to four yards of stretchy Lycra or spandex material (swimsuit material), needle and thread (or portable sewing machine)

Strategy

Tracing a Letter

Children with tactile sensitivity benefit the most from this activity.

Objective

To help children use touch to reinforce letter/shape knowledge

When to Use This Strategy

When you want to encourage the child to trace the shape of a letter or a number in a way that will not offend his sense of touch

Materials Needed

A sandwich-size plastic bag (freezer quality), inexpensive hair gel, heavy tape such as duct tape or electrical tape, cutout letters

What to Do

1. Fill a plastic bag with liquid hair gel. Hair gel comes in a variety of colors and can be found in large bottles in most discount stores.
2. This activity works best if you use a clear plastic freezer-quality bag. Regular sandwich bags are not durable enough and are likely to puncture easily.
3. Seal the bag and reinforce the seal with duct tape or other heavy tape.
4. Place the bag over a cutout letter and encourage the child to trace the letter with her finger through the bag.
5. Place several bags in the literacy/writing center. Write letters, names, or other words on index cards. Encourage children to trace their names or other cutout letters with their fingers.

Helpful Hints

◆ Fill the bag with blue hair gel and ask children to draw fish and seaweed on the bag with markers. You have an instant ocean!

◆ Use bags filled with hair gel to provide opportunities to trace other things such as shapes or numbers.

Monster Shapes

This strategy is helpful for encouraging children to explore new shapes and textures.

What to Do

1. Pre-cut shapes in a variety of colors, shapes, and sizes. Use items with different textures, such as cardboard, artist craft foam, construction paper, and cloth.

2. Give each child a piece of large paper or poster board and a glue stick. (Children with autism will often use a glue stick when they will not use glue.)

3. Tell the children that you are going to create monsters from the various shapes on the table. It's fine if you want to model for them how to put shapes together to make the monster, but avoid making a pattern for them to copy.

4. The child may want to arrange his monster shapes on the paper before he starts to glue. After the child has glued his monster together, allow time to dry.

5. Return to the project later and add details with crayons or markers. Encourage the child to give his monster a name.

Helpful Hints

◆ Display the monsters in the classroom.

◆ Try a clothesline show where all monsters are hung with clothespins.

Objective

To experiment with a variety of shapes and colors

When to Use This Strategy

When you want to help children experiment with a variety of different shapes and to tolerate various textures

Materials Needed

Materials with different textures, such as cardboard of varying thickness, artist craft foam squares, cloth of various colors and textures; construction paper; scissors; glue or gluestick; uncut poster board

Make and Shake

For a child who is extremely sensitive to touch, try covering her container with soft, fur-like material or velvet.

Objective

To help the child work on auditory (listening) skills

When to Use This Strategy

When you want to encourage the child to use her listening skills and when you want to help develop attention skills

Materials Needed

Plastic containers, such as oatmeal cans or Pringles™ cans; brightly-colored cloth; bowls of various materials, such as aquarium rocks, uncooked rice, dried beans, sunflower seeds, and sand; large spoons or scoops (coffee scoops work best), glue

What to Do

1. Gather enough plastic containers so each child has one. Oatmeal cans or Pringles™ cans work best.
2. Give the children scraps of brightly colored paper or cloth, and encourage each child to decorate his container with crayons. For a child who will not or cannot decorate the outside of her container, an alternative is to encourage her to decorate paper, and cover her container with the decorated paper.
3. Once the children have decorated their containers, take them to a table where you have set up bowls of various materials, including aquarium rocks, uncooked rice, sunflower seeds, sand, and dried beans.
4. Using the scoop provided, each child fills her container with one or more items.
5. When a child has filled her container with a combination she likes, ask her to close the lid and shake it gently. It is easier to add more now rather than trying to add more after you have glued the container shut.
6. Glue the lids to the containers and allow them to dry.
7. When the containers are dry, the children take turns shaking each other's container.
8. Ask the children to guess what is making the noise in each one.

Helpful Hint

◆ If you want to tone down the container's noise level, stick straight pins into the container before it is decorated. Put at least 30 pins around various parts of the container. (Make sure the children can't get to the pins!) When the child shakes it, the sound will be softer.

Help, I Can't Grasp It!

Watch the child and observe what his interests are. Children are more likely to use a book that is about something they enjoy.

What to Do

1. Many children do not have the fine motor skills to turn the slick pages of a book. Simple adaptations can enable the child to turn the pages more easily.

2. To make a temporary page-turner, attach a clothespin to each page, either on the top or side of the page, to make it easy for the child to grasp.

3. Permanent page turners can be made by putting a dot of hot glue in the upper right corner of each page. This will separate the pages and make the pages easier to turn.

Objective

To help the child develop fine motor skills

When to Use This Strategy

When you have determined that the child has difficulty with fine motor skills

Materials Needed

Clothespins, hot-glue gun (adult only), large paper clips, books

Helpful Hints

◆ Select books that are large enough for the child to hold easily.
◆ Color is nice, but avoid books with too much detail.

Strategy

STRATEGIES TO HELP CHILDREN WHO HAVE SENSORY INTEGRATION DISORDER

Make a Fidgety-Widgety Toy

Learning to regulate her own behavior is a very important step in the child's overall social and emotional development.

Objective

To help the child remain calm

When to Use This Strategy

When the child needs to calm down or while she is sitting in a group

Materials Needed

Deflated helium-type balloon; plastic sack; filler, such as flour, sand, or oatmeal; soft cloth or material; tape

What to Do

1. The fidgety-widgety is simply a toy that the child squeezes when she wants to remain calm.
2. To make it, fill a deflated helium-quality balloon or a sturdy, resealable plastic bag with flour, sand, or oatmeal.
3. Tie the end of the balloon or seal the plastic bag. If using a plastic bag, place it inside another plastic bag for added safety.
4. Cover the balloon or bag with soft cloth and seal the end.
5. Introduce the toy to the child and demonstrate how to squeeze it. Encourage the child to squeeze it, too.

6. Place the toy in a place that is easily accessible to the child.
7. When the ingredients in the fidgety-widgety begin to wear out, it can be replaced easily.

Helpful Hints

- Experiment with various textures, colors, and sizes.
- Make the toy small enough that the child can hold it in her hand.
- The fidgety-widgety is not designed to be a chew toy and should only be used in the presence of an adult.

Step With Me

This strategy is less effective if the child is overly tired or when there are too many children present.

What to Do

1. Trace each child's footprint. Use as many different colors of paper as possible.
2. Cut out each footprint and attach it to the floor. Place the footprints at various distances apart.
3. Invite the children to step on the footprints.
4. For added variety, if a child steps outside the footprints, he can go to the end of the line and start again.

Helpful Hints

◆ Try doing the activity to music.
◆ After the children have gotten used to human footprints, vary the game by adding paw prints or dinosaur prints.

Objective

To help the child practice and control his balance

When to Use This Strategy

When you want to help the child with his sense of balance, while encouraging small-group interaction

Materials Needed

Construction paper or tagboard, markers, scissors, tape

Strategy

Cocoon

Children who do not like to be touched are often very comfortable with the deep pressure involved in this activity.

Objective

To help the child relax by applying deep pressure to his body

When to Use This Strategy

When you want to provide the child with deep pressure before or just after an activity that involves stimulation of the senses, especially the sense of touch

Materials Needed

Foam-type mat, lightweight sleeping bag, or rubber gym mat; a large, sturdy beach ball or therapy ball

What to Do

1. Play a game with the child. Using deep even pressure, press the ball up and down the child's body. Say something like, "We're pretending you are a worm. We need to get you ready for your cocoon."
2. Say to the child, "Tell me when you want me to stop." Pause and see if the child responds.
3. Next say, "Are you ready to get in your cocoon?" Gently, but firmly, roll the child up in the mat or sleeping bag. This is best accomplished by putting one hand on the child's shoulder and the other hand on his hip or leg.
4. Rock the child back and forth a few times.
5. When you have determined that the child is ready to quit, say, "Now we are going to pretend you are a butterfly."
6. Gently, unroll the child by grasping the edge of the mat. If possible, encourage the child to unroll himself while you hold firmly to the mat.

Helpful Hints

◆ This activity can be a fun and relaxing way to help the child cope with sensory overload.
◆ If the child does not want his whole body in the cocoon, try just his torso, hands, or feet.
◆ Safety is always the most important consideration. Never cover a child's head when rolling him up in the mat, and always remember that this activity requires adult supervision.

Stand-Up Pushups!

This strategy serves as a way for the child to calm himself before he goes into sensory overload.

What to Do

1. Select a large, solid structure in the room or on the playground. A wall or a permanent structure works best.
2. Walk up to the wall and say, "I'm going to do some stand-up pushups."
3. Place your hands against the wall and count to 10.
4. Use varying amounts of pressure and smile at the child while you push against the wall.
5. Invite the child to join you in a stand-up pushup.
6. To encourage interaction, invite other peers to join in the fun.

Helpful Hints

◆ Remember, this activity requires adult supervision.
◆ Encourage the child to try this with other parts of his body as well, such as his hips, back, or using his feet while lying down.

Objective

To help the child calm down and transition from one activity to another

When to Use This Strategy

When the child needs assistance with his body position (proprioceptive system)

Materials Needed

None

Products for Children With Sensory Integration Disorders

Abilitations
3155 Northwoods Parkway
Norcross, GA 30071
www.abilitations.com

Southpaw Enterprises
PO Box 1047
Dayton, OH 45401
www.Southpawenterprises.com

Sensory Resources
2500 Chandler Avenue, Suite 3
Las Vegas, NV 89120-4064
www.sensoryresources.com

Special Needs Toys
4537 Gibsonia Road
Gibsonia, PA 15044
www.Specialneedstoys.com

Resources Used in This Chapter

Hanbury, M. 2005. *Educating pupils with autistic spectrum disorders: A practical guide*. London: Paul Chapman Publishing.

Kluth, P. 2003. *You're going to love this kid!: Teaching students with autism in the inclusive classroom*. Baltimore: Paul H. Brookes Publishing Co.

Kranowitz, C.S. 2003. *The out-of-sync child has fun: Safe activities for home and school—sensory-motor, appropriate, fun, and easy*. New York: The Berkley Publishing Group.

Kranowitz, C.S. 2005. *The out-of-sync child: Recognizing and coping with sensory integration dysfunction*. New York: Penguin Group.

Murray-Slutsky, C. & Paris, B.A. 2001. *Exploring the spectrum of autism and pervasive developmental disorders: Intervention strategies*. New York: Elsevier Science.

Yee, C.E. (n.d.). *How to know if it's sensory/What to do?* Retrieved August 2, 2005, from http://www.autism-pdd.net

Key Terms

Hypersensitive: Overly sensitive to sensory stimulation.

Hyposensitive: Under-sensitive to sensory stimulation.

Proprioceptive sense: The sense that receives information from joints, muscles, and ligaments, providing information about where parts of the body are and what they are doing.

Sensory Integration Dysfunction (SI Dysfunction): A condition resulting from an insufficient process in the brain, whereby a child is unable to analyze and respond appropriately to the information received from the senses.

Vestibular sense: The sense that provides information through the inner ear about balance, movement (inner ear) and gravity.

We're All In This **Together!**

Teaming Up With Families

What Can I Do to Understand a Family's Perspective?

Unless you have a child with disabilities, you can never truly understand the perspective of parents who do. You can sympathize and try to appreciate how parents might feel, but you can never really know the day-to-day realities of living with and caring for a child with disabilities.

For parents of a child with autism, their child is not just an autistic child. He or she is special, and is a valued

Make every child feel part of the classroom community.

member of their family. Helen, the mother of Nathan, a child with autism, puts it this way:

> *"When Nathan was created, there was a microscopic change, which occurred randomly in nature. We don't know why it happened and we didn't cause it to happen…we've always tried to do our best with him, even if it was not what his therapists thought we should be doing. Please remember, Nathan is valued by his family… he is a joy and a gift. In fact, when he was almost a year old, we discovered the name Nathan means 'Gift from God'."*

When working with parents, it is best if the teacher can appreciate that parents of a child with a disability are doing the best they can with the resources they have at that given time.

As a teacher, your job is to help every child in your care become part of the classroom community. You know from experience that all children have strengths and challenges. Some children just happen to have more challenges than others. Parents often agree that the one thing that a teacher can do to understand their perspective is to be respectful of their opinions and treat them as valued contributors. When you first meet with them, parents are usually aware that they have a child who is not like other children. They have likely seen more than one specialist and scoured the Internet searching for information about autism. They may have accessed an Internet list-serv or visited chat rooms designed for parents of children with autism. A few may be lucky enough to be involved in parent support groups. Regardless of how much they already know, parents are always seeking more explanations and answers about what they can do to help their child. Teachers can help parents by making sure they know about resources that may be available to them.

Resources may include:
♦ Access to specialists such as occupational therapists or speech/language pathologists.

Involve everyone who works with the child in a team meeting.

- Information about local support groups for families.
- Suggestions about where they might go to obtain adaptive equipment or specialized materials for their child.
- Names of community organizations that provide financial support for children with disabilities.
- Government resources that they may be entitled to receive.
- Where to locate respite care (a place where the child can go for a day or a few days, so the parents can have a break).
- Organizations that specialize in autism, such as the Autism Society of America (http://www.autism-society.org).
- Programs designed to provide more information about autism.

Disability literature is full of information about the value of enabling and empowering families to become self-advocates. When you enable a family, you give them the tools they need to make informed decisions; when you empower them, you show them how to use those tools. What this means is that you become an avenue through which parents learn to use the resources and tools available to them in order to advocate for what is in the best interest of their child. At the end of this chapter, you will find a resource list that provides help for families to locate information they need.

It is important to note that, at various times in the life of a child with autism, his family experiences a cycle of grief and loss that is not unlike what is experienced when an immediate family member dies. Determining where a parent is functioning within that cycle at the time the child enters your classroom provides a better understanding of that parent's point of view.

What Is the Cycle of Grief and Loss?

The grieving process that a family experiences when they discover their child has a disability or disorder has been compared to the grieving process that is associated with the death of a close relative. This process includes shock, denial, anger, despair, and ultimately, acceptance.

Parents of children with disabilities never forget about their initial shock at being told their child has a disability. Articles written by parents of children with disabilities relate the circumstances under which they received the news. In the past, such news was often delivered in a clinical setting with little regard for the feelings of the family, where questions about the prognosis for the child or how to best treat the child were often answered with medical jargon that parents did not understand. Today, many parents report that their initial diagnosis was given in a very loving and supportive manner by a caring professional who

Teachers can help parents by making sure they know about resources that may be available to them.

answered their questions with information they could use. In many cases, from the moment a diagnosis is received, parents have access to counselors and health care professionals who help them cope with the diagnosis.

No matter how gently a parent is told about their child's disability, it is always a shock. Unlike most childhood illnesses that are cured with medication or therapy, families must face a situation that is chronic. Brian, the father of a child with autism, related the following, "We walked outside after hearing that Billy has autism, and people were walking to their cars, the sun was shining, and the world looked so normal. How could it all look the same? Our lives would never be the same again!"

After the initial shock begins to wear off, many parents move into a phase known as denial. During this phase, the family is finding out that their perfect child, their gift, has something wrong with him. This is especially difficult for families of children with autism, because often that diagnosis takes months or years to obtain. While one or both parents may feel that something is not quite right with their child, it is not until a diagnosis is confirmed that they begin to face the reality of life with a child with disabilities.

It is not uncommon at this point for a parent who has been given a diagnosis to seek out multiple opinions. In fact, one or both parents may begin to shop for a cure. That means that they search for anyone or anything that might fix the problem. Families are particularly vulnerable when they first learn their child has a disability and may become victimized by people who prey on their desire to find a cure. Some families have taken out a second or even a third mortgage on their home to pay for these cures. After exhausting all their financial resources, they find that there is no magic pill to cure autism.

During the next phase, parents begin to experience strong emotions, such as anger and despair, and may feel the need to blame someone for the child's disabilities. It is not uncommon to experience a feeling that we are in this alone and a sometimes overwhelming anger at the stressful situation or circumstance in which they find themselves. It is during this phase that marriages end, and, as a result, families may begin to face great difficulty and begin to fall apart. One spouse may blame the other for not spending more time at home or not accepting enough responsibility for the child. Self-blame is also common, as a parent (usually the mother) feels that she did something wrong during pregnancy that caused the child to have autism. Brandy, the mother of a six-year-old with autism says, "I keep going over and over the things I did when I was pregnant. I painted the baby's room, I pumped my own gas, I had the stomach flu... Did any of these things cause Lee's autism? Did I cause him to be this way?"

Ultimately, most families come to accept the disability as being a part of who the child is and learn to appreciate the child for what he can do rather than what he cannot do. Yet, as the child reaches various milestones in his life (starting school, reaching puberty, and so on), families may revisit one or part of the cycle again. Regardless of where parents are functioning within the cycle of grief and loss, or what might be taking place at home, teachers still need their help for the child to have a positive experience in the classroom.

How Do I Let Parents Know I Need Their Help?

As soon as you discover that you will have a child with autism in your class, begin to communicate with his family. From the very first moment, when you meet them, use language that shows how you want them to be part of a team whose sole purpose is to plan for what is best for their child.

Treat parents as team members.

For example:

◆ Use words like "we" and "us" instead of "me" and "you."

◆ Talk about their child's strengths and challenges.

◆ Ask them what they think, and then respect what they say.

◆ Use the child's name when you talk about him.

◆ Ask about the family's priorities. What would they like to see him accomplish this year?

◆ Always look for ways to help make all interactions with families a positive experience for both you and the family.

What Can I Do To Make Family Interactions Positive?

Although there are many types of families from various circumstances and with different issues, interactions with them can be positive and successful. To facilitate good interactions, it is important to do the following throughout the process:

◆ Plan ahead.

◆ Develop rapport by being respectful and attentive to what families say.

◆ Foster a sense of trust.

◆ Communicate frequently.

◆ Acknowledge and value input when it is given.

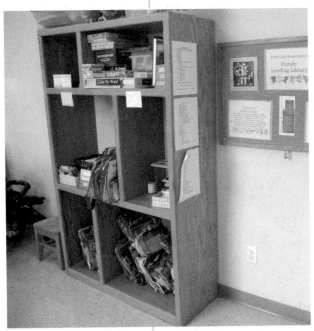

A family lending
library

Planning ahead means that you schedule conferences and meetings in advance and at a time that is convenient for the family. This helps relieve their added stress of losing time from work, finding a babysitter, or in some cases finding someone to bring them to the meeting. Keep conferences short, and try to avoid lengthy discussions about everything the child is not doing. If possible, write an agenda for the meeting and allow a set amount of time for each team member to give input. If parents know the purpose of the meeting ahead of time, they can come better prepared. Give the agenda to the parent who will be at the conference.

Be sure to start the conference by telling the parent at least one positive thing about their child. It will not only set the tone for the whole conference, but it lets parents know that you are there for more than just telling them about problems with their child. Review the role they play in their child's program.

The relationship that you build with the family depends on the rapport that you are able to establish. By respecting the needs and desires of the family, you are indicating that you value their input. Even though you may have a difference of opinion about some aspect of the child's education, you can still share information with each other openly and honestly. Once you establish rapport with a child's family, it will be easier to discuss his needs and make plans to address those needs. Rapport leads to relationships, and relationships help build trust.

Before parents will trust you, they must be able to see that you are worthy of their trust. They want to know that you are concerned about their child's well-being and development and will take the steps necessary to create a positive environment for their child. It does not come easily or quickly. Once a level of trust is established, you are well on your way to being able to make decisions that are in the best interest of the child. Again, the purpose of this book is to help better prepare you for this.

Communicate with parents often and in a variety of ways. Communication provides an on-going association with them, as well as strengthening their confidence regarding their child's experience and progress. A communication notebook that is sent home regularly with the child can be a great method for you to tell parents what is going on at school and for parents to tell you what is going on at home. Imagine how much easier it will be at school, if you know

TEACHING YOUNG CHILDREN WITH AUTISM

ahead of time that the child did not sleep well the night before, or that he is anxious because one of his parents is going on a long business trip.

How Does All of This Fit Together?

Let's look at an example of a parent interaction:

Kevin lives with his mother, Martha, and his brother, Cameron. When Kevin was three, he was diagnosed with autism. His family went through the "cycle of grief." By the time Kevin's fourth birthday rolled around, although his parents were divorced, they had come to grips with his disability. Martha had resumed her career as a dental assistant and enrolled Kevin in a local preschool. The first two weeks of school were anything but pleasant. From the moment he arrived at school, Kevin was frightened and upset. He had violent tantrums and could not adjust to his new routine. He refused to eat at school, and at least once a day, urinated in his pants. The teacher called his mother at work to advise her that she should come in for a conference as soon as possible. After a long day at work, Martha arrives at Kevin's preschool angry and upset. The first words out of her mouth are, "What has he done this time?"

The teacher thinks to herself, "All I need today is an angry parent!" and tells Martha that unless she puts Kevin back in diapers, he may not be able to stay in her classroom. Martha grabs Kevin and heads for the door, as she says, "You don't want him here! So, I'll just find some place that does!" The teacher reports to her director that Martha is a parent who can't accept her child's disability.

It is always important to use a team approach and strive to make family interactions positive.

Unfortunately, this situation could have had a much better ending had Kevin's teacher been a little more prepared. First, instead of calling Martha at work and demanding that she come in for a conference, perhaps a note sent home asking her to come into school at her earliest convenience might have set a different tone for the meeting. The teacher may even have prefaced the note with a statement such as, "Martha, we need to develop some strategies to help Kevin adjust to his new school."

Second, when Martha arrived and asked, "What has he done this time?" the teacher should have tuned into the frustration in her voice and immediately made a comment that did not put Martha on the defensive. Imagine how the situation might have turned out differently, with the teacher saying, "Martha, you look like you've had a rough day, can I get you a soft drink or a glass of water? Sit down and relax a minute, while we figure out what we can do to help Kevin let us know when he needs to go to the potty." Rather than making Martha feel like she was at fault, the teacher took a team approach and focused the discussion on Kevin and his needs. To make a child's experience in your classroom one that is meaningful to him and his family, it is always important to use a team approach and strive to make family interactions positive.

The following excerpts are reprinted with permission from an article that was published in *Our Voice*, the Autism Network International newsletter, in 1993. Although the information was written several years ago, and primarily for parents, there is a lesson here for all who strive to make life better for children with autism.

> *Parents often report that learning their child is autistic was the most traumatic thing that ever happened to them. Non-autistic people see autism as a great tragedy, and parents experience continuing disappointment and grief at all stages of the child's and family's life cycle.*

> *But this grief does not stem from the child's autism in itself. It is grief over the loss of the normal child the parents had hoped and expected to have... I invite you to look at our autism, and look at your grief, from our perspective...*

> *Autism isn't something a person has, or a "shell" that a person is trapped inside. There's no normal child hidden behind the autism. Autism is a way of being. It is pervasive; it colors every experience, every sensation, perception, thought, emotion, and encounter, every aspect of existence. It is not possible to separate the autism from the person—and if it were possible, the person you'd have left would not be the same person you started with...* (Sinclair, 1993)

Resources for Families

Websites for Parents

Autism Research Institute: www.AutismResearchInstitute.com

Autism Society of America: www.autism-society.org

Cure Autism Now: www.cureautismnow.org

OAR-Organization for autism research: www.autismorg.com

Advice To Parents Who Have Just Found Out Their Child Has Autism:
www.autism-resources.com/advice-to-parents.html
www.autism.org/adviceforparents.html

Books for Parents

Harris, S.L., & M.J. Weiss. 1998. *Right from the start: Behavioral intervention for young children with autism—A guide for parents and professionals.* Bethesda, MD: Woodbine House Publishers.

Henriques, L. & P. Abrams. 2004.*The Autistic Spectrum parents' daily helper: A workbook for you and your child.* Berkley, CA: Ulysses Press.

Janzen, J.E. 1999. *Autism: Facts and strategies for parents.* San Antonio, TX: Therapy Skill Builders.

Sigman, M. & Capps, L. 1997. *Children with autism: A developmental perspective.* Cambridge, MA: Harvard University Press.

Resources Used in This Chapter

Sinclair, J. 1993. *Don't mourn for us. Our Voice: the newsletter of the Autism Network International,* 1(3). Retrieved from http://ani.autistics.org/dont_mourn.html

Key Terms

Adaptive equipment: Equipment that has been modified or changed so a person with disabilities can use it more effectively.

Cycle of grief and loss: The cycle experienced when someone dies. This process includes shock, denial, anger, despair, and ultimately, acceptance.

Occupational therapist: A specialist who helps the child learn to perform daily tasks required to be independent.

Respite care: A place where the child can go for a day or a few days, so the primary caregivers can have a break.

Speech/language pathologist: A specialist who helps the child in the areas of speech, language, and/or communication.

Glossary of Terms

Adaptive equipment: Equipment which has been modified or changed so that a person with disabilities can use it more effectively.

Aggression: Behavior that is harmful to others, such as biting, hitting, slapping, kicking, pinching, or pulling hair.

Alternative Communication System: A method of communication that does not involve speech.

Anecdotal record: Ongoing notes made by the teacher concerning a child's behavior or performance of a task.

Approximation: An inexact representation of a skill or a word that is still close enough to be useful.

Attend: To pay attention to or to concentrate.

Augmentative forms of communication: An alternative way to communicate, such as a device that speaks for the child.

Autism Spectrum Disorder (ASD): Autism Spectrum Disorder (ASD) is a broad term which includes the classical form of autism as well as several related disabilities that share many of the same characteristics including difficulty with communication, socialization and behavior. It is called spectrum because autism and autism-related characteristics range from very mild to very severe.

Autism: A complex developmental disability that typically appears during the first three years of life. To be diagnosed with autism, a person must demonstrate either delayed or atypical behaviors in at least one of three categories: interaction, communication, or behavior.

Beta-endorphin: A chemical in the brain that helps the body calm down and relax.

Casein: A protein found in food that contains wheat, rye, oats, barley and dairy products.

Challenging behavior: A problem behavior defined as any action where the child deliberately hurts himself, injures others, and/or causes damage to his environment.

Communication: An interaction between two or more people where information is exchanged.

Communicative replacement: A form of communication or a message that the child gives to you that replaces the behavior.

Compulsive: Behaviors the child performs repeatedly that will be stopped and begun again, if a certain step is not performed exactly the same way every time.

Control sentence: Control sentences are used in social stories and serve as a cue or hint, to remind the child how to react in a social setting.

Cue: A hint that is a word, gesture, or phrase.

Cycle of grief and loss: The cycle experienced when someone dies. This process includes shock, denial, anger, despair, and ultimately, acceptance.

Descriptive sentence: Type of sentence used in social stories to address who, what, where, and why of the social situation.

Developmentally appropriate practices: Activities and educational experiences that match the child's age and stage of development.

Directive sentence: Type of sentence used in social stories to tell the child how to respond to a situation. It suggests a specific action on the part of the child that will enhance the social interaction.

Echolalia: The echoing and repetition of a phrase or word.

Egocentric: Self-absorbed, believing the world revolved around them.

Electronic communication device: Sometimes called an augmentative communication device; a mechanical device that is designed to talk for the child, when it is activated either by a switch or by pressing a button.

Expressive communication: How the child inputs his message to the person receiving it. The method used to communicate with others.

Food jag: When the child will only eat certain foods. Some food jags are preferential, in that while they prefer one food to other foods, the child will eat non-preferred foods. Other food jags are more absolute, in that the child will only eat certain foods to the exclusion of all others.

Form: The way a child behaves. Examples of forms of behavior are hitting, biting, and so on.

Free and Appropriate Public Education (FAPE): Special education law is clear that a child with disabilities is entitled to an education that is free and appropriate for his individual needs.

Function: The reason why something happens. The function of a behavior is the reason behind the behavior.

Functional assessment: An evaluation designed to determine the relationship between events in a child's environment and the occurrence of challenging behaviors.

Functional skills: Everyday skills that the child will use to be more independent, sometimes called self-help or independent living skills. Functional skills are the skills a child will use throughout his life such as brushing his teeth, going to the bathroom and taking a bath.

Generalization: Being able to perform the same task, skill, or activity in a variety of settings or with a variety of people and/or different objects.

Gluten: A protein found in food that contains wheat, rye, oats, barley, and dairy products.

Hypersensitive: Overly sensitive to something. The state of being overly stimulated by the environment.

Hyposensitive: Under-sensitive to sensory stimulation.

Imaginative play: Play activities that involve using imagination.

Individual Education Plan (IEP): A personalized plan for a child designed by a team including the child's parents which outlines the educational goals and objectives for the child over a period of time (usually one school year).

Individual Family Service Plan (IFSP): A written plan for services a child will receive, to help guide the family as the child transitions into other programs. The IFSP is written for children birth to three. Once a child turns three, an IEP is written if he still qualifies for special education services.

Individuals with Disabilities Education Act (IDEA): (Public Law 101-476) IDEA outlines very specific guidelines that local school districts are required by law to adhere to when providing for the needs of children with disabilities.

Intentional communication: Communication that is on purpose or deliberate.

Language disorder: A deficit in using words or vocabulary. It can also involve how a child understands language and uses it in social settings.

Learned helplessness: When a child learns how to be helpless because he never has the opportunity to do anything for himself; instead, everything is done for him.

Least restrictive environment: Under the IDEA all children who require special education services must be educated in the setting that is most appropriate to their individual needs.

Life-skills: Self-help skills, such as going to the bathroom or washing hands.

Maladaptive behavior: A behavior that is not common in most children or one that is so severe that it interferes with learning.

Natural consequence: The logical result of an action.

Natural environment: The place where the child might spend most of her time if she did not have a disability.

Non-functional communication: Communication that lacks meaning or purpose.

Obsession: A strong inclination toward something to the point of excluding everything else, such as collecting forks or watching the blades of a rotating ceiling fan.

Occupational therapist: A specialist who helps the child learn to perform daily tasks required to be independent.

Parallel play: Play, where one child plays near or beside another child and may even share some of the same toys, but they do not play together in a reciprocal fashion.

Peer buddy: Someone who is assigned to interact and play with a child for a given period.

People-first language: Referring to the person, and then the disability.

Perceptive communication: How the child receives messages or information from others.

Personal space: The space in which someone feels comfortable: their comfort zone.

Perspective sentence: Type of sentence used in social stories to provide information about the thoughts, feelings, and emotions of others.

Picture apron: An apron worn by the teacher with pictures depicting the day's schedule.

Picture schedule: A series of pictures showing what is supposed to occur within an area or time-frame.

Portfolio: A collection of the child's best work across a specific period. The portfolio is not intended to represent all the child's work; it should showcase a child's best efforts across specific domains.

Positron Emission Tomography (PET): Medical testing that looks at the electrical energy within the brain to determine what part of the brain is responsible for certain actions and behaviors.

Pragmatic language: Involves using language in a social setting. For example, knowing what is appropriate to say, when to say it, and the general give and take nature of a friendly conversation.

Pretend play: Make-believe play.

Proactive: A procedure or action that happens before a problem occurs and is designed to prevent the problem or behavior from occurring.

Proprioceptive sense: The sense that receives information from joints, muscles, and ligaments, and provides information about where parts of the body are and what they are doing.

Reciprocal play: Direct play with a partner where the children interact with each other.

Respite care: A place where the child can go for a day or a few days, so the primary caregivers can have a break.

Reverse chaining: When a child starts at the end of an activity and does the process in reverse. For example, when you are trying to get a child to learn to put on his coat, in reverse chaining you would start with taking off the coat.

Ritual: A pattern or way of doing something that is not logical, such as only walking on the floor instead of carpet or having to arrange food in a certain order before it can be eaten.

Ritualistic: Following a set pattern or routine without variation.

Self-injurious behavior: Something a child does to hurt herself in an effort to get out of a situation or an environment that is overwhelming, such as hitting or biting herself.

Sensory Integration Disorder: An inability to filter or screen out sensory-related input.

Sensory Integration Dysfunction (SI Dysfunction): A condition resulting from an insufficient process in the brain, whereby a child is unable to analyze and respond appropriately to the information received from the senses.

Serotonin: A hormone found in the brain. It acts as a chemical messenger that transmits signals between nerve cells. Changes in the serotonin levels in the brain can affect mood and behavior. Serotonin is also found in blood platelets, and the digestive tract.

Setting event: Conditions that occur at the same time a challenging behavior occurs.

Social story: A strategy designed by Carol Gray in which stories are used to help children with autism learn social interaction skills in the context of a story.

Socialization: The ability to get along with others.

Socially avoidant: A type of social impairment characterized by a child who tries to escape social situations.

Socially awkward: A type of social impairment characterized by a child who does not understand the give and take nature of a social interaction.

Socially competent: By definition, a socially competent child has developed strong interpersonal communication skills, knows how to form relationships with peers, and understands the value of appropriately interacting with others.

Socially indifferent: A type of social impairment characterized by a child who is indifferent to social situations.

Solitary play: Playing alone or play that does not involve others.

Speech/language pathologist: A specialist who helps the child in the areas of speech, language, and/or communication.

Stereotypic behavior: A behavior that is carried out repeatedly and involves either movement of the child's body or movement of an object, such as repetitive hand flapping or saying the same phrase repeatedly.

Symbolic play: Using one object or toy to represent another, such as pretending a square block is a camera or that a cardboard box is a jet plane.

Talking stick: A sealed, decorated tube with items inside that make interesting sounds.

Tantrum: Anger beyond what is normally seen in children, such as falling to the floor and screaming or throwing their bodies on the ground.

Task analysis: The breaking down of a skill into steps; step-by-step guide.

Transition: Moving from one activity or area in the classroom to another.

Typically developing: A child who is developing at a rate similar to his peers; a term often used to describe a child without disabilities.

Urinary Peptide Test: A medical test to detect protein that is not fully broken down and digested by the body.

Vestibular sense: The sense that provides information through the inner ear about balance, movement, and gravity.

References

Abrams, P. & L. Henriques. 2004. *The autistic spectrum: Parent's daily helper.* Berkeley, CA: Ulysses Press.

Atwood, T. 1993. *Why does Chris do that?* London: National Autism Society.

Baker, B. L., & A. J. Brightman. 2003. *Steps to independence: Teaching everyday skills to children with special needs.* Baltimore, MD: Paul H. Brookes Publishing Co.

Baker, Bruce L., & A.J. Brightman. 2004. *Steps to independence: Teaching everyday skills to children with special needs (4th edition).* Baltimore, MD: Paul H. Brookes Publishing Co.

Baker, J.E. 2001. *The social skills picture book: Teaching play, emotion and communication to children with autism.* Arlington, TX: Future Horizons, Inc.

Baker, J. E. 2003. *Social skills training: For children and adolescents with Asperger syndrome and social-communication problems.* Shawnee Mission, KS: Autism Asperger Publishing Company.

Bondy, A. & L. Frost. 2002. *A picture's worth: PECS and other visual communication strategies in autism.* Bethesda, MD: Woodbine House.

Buie, Timothy. 2005. *Treating autism in children: Neuro-gastroenterology and autism.* A paper presented at Harvard University: Learning and the Brain Conference (12th Conference), Cambridge, MA.

Cohen, S. 1998. *Targeting autism.* Berkley, CA: University of California Press.

Cohen, S. 2002. *Targeting autism: What we know, don't know, and can do to help young children with autism and related disorders.* Berkley, CA: University of California Press.

Fouse, B. & M. Wheeler. 1997. *A treasure chest of behavioral strategies for individuals with autism.* Arlington, TX: Future Horizons.

Gillingham, G. 2000. *Autism a new understanding.* Edmonton, Alberta, Canada: Tacit Publishing, Inc.

Gutstein, S. E. & R. Sheely. 2002. *Relationship development intervention with young children: Social and emotional development activities for Asperger syndrome, autism, PDD and NLD.* London: Jessica Kingsley Publishers.

Hanbury, M. 2005. *Educating pupils with autistic spectrum disorders: A practical guide.* London: Paul Chapman Publishing.

Harris, S. L., & M. J. Weiss. 1998. *Right from the start: Behavioral Intervention for young children with autism.* Bethesda, MD: Woodbine House.

Isbell, C. & R. Isbell. 2005. *The inclusive learning center book for preschool children with special needs.* Beltsville, MD: Gryphon House, Inc.

Janzen, J. E. 2003. *Understanding the nature of autism: A guide to the autism spectrum disorders.* San Antonio, TX: Therapy Skill Builders.

Janzen, J. E., & Therapy Skills Builders. 2000. *Autism: Facts and strategies for parents.* New York: Elsevier Science.

Johnson, M. D., & S.H. Corden. 2004. *Beyond words the successful inclusion of a child with autism.* Knoxville, TN: Merry Pace Press.

Kluth, P. 2003. *You're going to love this kid!: Teaching students with autism in the inclusive classroom.* Baltimore, MD: Paul H. Brookes Publishing Co.

Kranowitz, C.S. 2003. *The out-of-sync child has fun: Safe activities for home and school—sensory-motor, appropriate, fun, and easy.* New York: The Berkley Publishing Group.

Kranowitz, C.S. 2005. *The out-of-sync child: Recognizing and coping with sensory integration dysfunction.* New York: Penguin Group.

Leaf, R. & J. McEachin, (Eds.). 1999. *A work in progress: Behavior management strategies and a curriculum for intensive behavioral treatment of autism.* New York: Autism Partnership

MacDonald, L. 2000. *Learning interrupted: Maladaptive behavior in the classroom.* Retrieved from http://www.mugsy.org

McCabe, P. & P. Meller. 2004. *The relationship between language and social competence: How language impairment affects social growth.* Psychology in the Schools, 41(3), 313-322.

McClannahan, L. E., & P.J. Krantz. 1998. *Activity schedules for children with autism: Teaching independent behavior.* Bethesda, MD: Woodbine House.

Moor, J. 2005. *Playing, laughing, and learning with children on the autism spectrum.* London: Jessica Kingsley Publishers.

Murray-Slutsky, C. & B.A. Paris. 2001. *Exploring the spectrum of autism and pervasive developmental disorders: Intervention strategies.* New York: Elsevier Science.

Schiller, P. 2002. *Start smart! Building brain power in the early years.* Beltsville, MD: Gryphon House, Inc.

Scott, J., C. Clark, & M.P. Brady. 1999. *Students with autism: Characteristics and instructional programming for special educators.* Belmont, CA: Wadsworth Publishing.

Sicile-Kira, C. 2004. *Autism spectrum disorders: The complete guide to understanding autism, Asperger's Syndrome, pervasive developmental disorder, and other ASDs.* New York: The Berkley Publishing Group.

Siegel, B. 2003. *Helping children with autism learn: Treatment approaches for parents and professionals.* New York: Oxford University Press.

Sigman, M. & L. Capps. 1997. *Children with autism: A developmental perspective.* Cambridge: Harvard University Press.

Sinclair, J. 1993. *Don't mourn for us. Our Voice: the newsletter of the Autism Network International,* 1(3). Retrieved from http://ani.autistics.org/dont_mourn.html

Small, M. & L. Kontente. 2003. *Everyday solutions: A practical guide for families of children with autism spectrum disorders.* Shawnee Mission, KS: Autism Asperger Publishing Company.

Sonders, S.A. 2002. *Giggle time—Establishing the social connection: a program to develop the communication skills of children with autism, Asperger's Syndrome and PDD.* London: Jessica Kingsley Publishers Ltd.

Strock, M. 2004. *Autism spectrum disorders (Pervasive Developmental Disorders).* Bethesda, MD: National Institute of Mental Health, National Institutes of Health, U.S. Department of Health and Human Services. (NIH Publication No. NIH-04-5511)

Sussman, F. 1999. *More than words: Helping parents promote communication and social skills in young children with autism spectrum disorder.* Toronto: The Hanen Centre.

Szatmari, P. 2004. *A mind apart: Understanding children with autism and Asperger's Syndrome.* New York: The Guilford Press.

Wall, K. 2004. *Autism and early years practice: A guide for early years professionals, teachers and parents.* London: Paul Chapman Publishing.

Wallin, J.M. 2005. *Social stories: An introduction to social stories.* Retrieved August 5, 2005, from http://www.polyxo.com/social stories/introduction.html

Weatherby, A. M., & B. Prizant. 2001. *Autism spectrum disorders: A transactional developmental perspective,* Vol. 9. Baltimore, MD: Paul H. Brookes Publishing Co.

Wheeler, Maria. 2004. *Toilet training for individuals with autism and related disorders: A comprehensive guide for parents and teachers.* Arlington, TX: Future Horizons.

Williams, D. 1996. *Autism: An inside-out approach: An innovative look at the mechanics of autism and its developmental cousins.* London: Jessica Kingsley Publishers.

Willis, C. 1998. *Language development: A key to lifelong learning. Child Care Information Exchange,* 121, 63-65.

Willis, C. 1999. *Brain research implications for caregivers and teachers. The Viewpoint.* The Virginia Association for Early Childhood Education, 2, 1-3.

Wolfberg, P. 2003. *Peer play and the autism spectrum: The art of guiding children's socialization and imagination.* Shawnee Mission, KS: Autism Asperger Publishing Company.

Yee, C.E. (n.d.). *How to know if it's sensory/What to do?* Retrieved August 2, 2005, from http://www.autism-pdd.net

Further Reading

Abrams, P. & L. Henriques. 2004. *The autistic spectrum: Parent's daily helper.* Berkeley, CA: Ulysses Press.

Atwood, T. 1993. *Why does Chris do that?* London: National Autism Society.

Baker, B. L., & A. J. Brightman. 2003. *Steps to independence: Teaching everyday skills to children with special needs.* Baltimore, MD: Paul H. Brookes Publishing Co.

Baker, J. E. 2001. *The social skills picture book: Teaching play, emotion and communication to children with autism.* Arlington, TX: Future Horizons, Inc.

Bondy, A. & L. Frost. 2002. *A picture's worth: PECS and other visual communication strategies in autism.* Bethesda, MD: Woodbine House.

Buron, K. D. 2003. *When my autism gets too big! A relaxation book for children with autism spectrum disorders.* Shawnee Mission, KS: Autism Asperger Publishing Company.

Cohen, S. 2002. *Targeting autism: What we know, don't know, and can do to help young children with autism and related disorders.* Berkley, CA: University of California Press.

Fouse, B. & M. Wheeler. 1997. *A treasure chest of behavioral strategies for individuals with autism.* Arlington, TX: Future Horizons.

Gillingham, G. 2000. *Autism: A new understanding.* Edmonton, Alberta, Canada: Tacit Publishing, Inc.

Hanbury, M. 2005. *Educating pupils with autistic spectrum disorders: A practical guide.* London: Paul Chapman Publishing.

Harris, S. L., & M.J. Weiss. 1998. *Right from the start: Behavioral Intervention for young children with autism.* Bethesda, MD: Woodbine House.

Isbell, C. & R. Isbell. 2005. *The inclusive learning center book for preschool children with special needs.* Beltsville, MD: Gryphon House, Inc.

Janzen, J. E. 2003. *Understanding the nature of autism: A guide to the autism spectrum disorders.* San Antonio, TX: Therapy Skill Builders.

Janzen, J. E., & Therapy Skills Builders. 2000. *Autism: Facts and strategies for parents.* New York: Elsevier Science.

Kluth, P. 2003. *You're going to love this kid!: Teaching students with autism in the inclusive classroom.* Baltimore, MD: Paul H. Brookes Publishing Co.

Kranowitz, C. S. 2005. *The out-of-sync child: Recognizing and coping with sensory integration dysfunction.* New York: Penguin Group.

Kranowitz, C. S. 2003. *The out-of-sync child has fun: Safe activities for home and school—sensory-motor, appropriate, fun, and easy.* New York: The Berkley Publishing Group.

McClannahan, L. E., & P. J. Krantz. 1998. *Activity schedules for children with autism: Teaching independent behavior.* Bethesda, MD: Woodbine House.

Moor, J. 2005. *Playing, laughing, and learning with children on the autism spectrum.* London: Jessica Kingsley Publishers.

Murray-Slutsky, C. & B. A. Paris. 2001. *Exploring the spectrum of autism and pervasive developmental disorders: Intervention strategies.* New York: Elsevier Science.

Sicile-Kira, C. 2004. *Autism spectrum disorders: The complete guide to understanding autism, Asperger's Syndrome, pervasive developmental disorder, and other ASDs.* New York: The Berkley Publishing Group.

Sigman, M. & L. Capps. 1997. *Children with autism: A developmental perspective.* Cambridge, MA: Harvard University Press.

Small, M. & L. Kontente. 2003. *Everyday solutions: A practical guide for families of children with autism spectrum disorders.* Shawnee Mission, KS: Autism Asperger Publishing Company.

Sonders, S. A. 2003. *Giggle time: Establishing the social connection.* London: Jessica Kingsley Publishers.

Sussman, F. 1999. *More than words: Helping parents promote communication and social skills in young children with autism spectrum disorder.* Toronto: The Hanen Centre.

Szatmari, P. 2004. *A mind apart: Understanding children with autism and Asperger Syndrome.* New York: The Guilford Press.

Wall, K. 2004. *Autism and early years practice: A guide for early years professionals, teachers and parents.* London: Paul Chapman Publishing.

Wallin, J.M. 2005. *Social stories: An introduction to social stories.* Retrieved August 5, 2005, from http://www.polyxo.com/social stories/introduction.html

Wheeler, M. 2004. *Toilet training for individuals with autism and related disorders: A comprehensive guide for parents and teachers.* Arlington, TX: Future Horizons.

Wolfberg, P. 2003. *Peer play and the autism spectrum.* Shawnee Mission, KS: Autism, Asperger Publishing Company.

Yee, C.E. (n.d.). *How to know if it's sensory/What to do?* Retrieved August 2, 2005, from http://www.autism-pdd.net.

Index

Crying, 16, 108, 113
Cue cards, 168
Cues, 41, 95
    defined, 207
    hands at home, 101
    musical, 46, 154
    over-stimulation, 102
    picture, 58–59, 126–127, 131, 147, 149
    social, 115, 158, 160
Cure Autism Now, 205
Curiosity, 148
Curriculum, 93
Cycle of grief and loss, 199–201
    defined, 205, 207

D

Dancing, 149, 181, 183
Deep breathing, 173
Deep pressure, 184, 194
Denial, 199–200, 205
Descriptive sentences, 163
    defined, 178, 207
Despair, 199–200, 205
Developmentally appropriate practices, 25, 207
Diarrhea, 36
Diet, 37
    food jags, 36
Directive sentences, 163
    defined, 178, 207
Display boards, 100
Distraction, 98–99, 170
Documentation
    anecdotal records, 38–40, 207
    communication notebooks, 131, 202–203
    portfolios, 37–38, 41, 177, 209
Dressing, 67
    resistance, 85
    teaching, 84–85

E

Ear covering, 185
Ear infections, 28–29
Ear pulling, 28–29
Early intervention, 20
    defined, 22
Echolalia, 17, 28, 39, 109–110, 113
    defined, 25, 134, 207
Egocentric, 158
    defined, 178, 207
Egocentric communication, 113
    goals for, 116
Electronic communication devices, 33, 121–122, 133
    defined, 134, 207
Eliciting attention, 28–29
Emerging communication, 114
    goals for, 116
Empathy, 157–158

Environment, 43–63
    adjusting to preschool, 55–54
    "all about me" board, 55–56
    books that teach stories, 57–58
    chaotic, 92
    consistency, 93
    curriculum, 93
    exploring new areas, 60
    familiarizing the classroom, 62
    fostering tolerance, 61
    from day one, 51–52
    lighting, 45, 47
    making friends, 58
    materials, 93
    modifying, 102
    morning greeting, 53–54
    natural, 21, 26, 66–67, 208
    over-stimulating, 34–35, 102
    picture schedules, 44–47, 53
    planning, 93
    predictable routines, 46–47
    preparing, 49–50
    pre-school visits, 43–44
    proactive, 92
    quiet centers, 45
    rules, 93
    school workers, 59
    transitions, 46
    welcoming all children, 47–48
Escape, 95, 161
Examples
    family/school partnerships, 203–204
    SI Disorder, 182
    teaching life skills, 68–69
Exploring the classroom, 60
Expressing feelings, 103
    communication notebooks, 131
Expressive communication, 111
    defined, 134, 207
Eye contact, 33, 58
Eye rubbing, 183
Eye-hand coordination, 180

F

Familiarizing the classroom, 62
Family/school partnerships, 14, 171, 197–205
    as school begins, 52
    asking parents' help, 201
    before school starts, 49–50
    case example, 203–204
    communication notebooks, 131, 202–203
    critical for success, 23–24
    defining priorities, 68, 71
    grief and loss, 199–201
    persistence, 176–177
    personal information, 81
    positive interactions, 201–203

New people, 165
Noise levels, 185, 190
Non-functional communication, 108–109
    defined, 134, 208
    function, 109
Nonsense speech, 39
Nontraditional families, 56
Nose holding, 183
Notebooks, 49, 56

O

OAR-Organization, 205
Observation, 162
    of play, 138–139
    SI Disorder, 181
Obsessions, 16, 19, 27–28, 39
    defined, 41, 208
    no function, 30
    reasons for, 30
Occupational therapists, 21, 197
    defined, 205, 207
One-to-one correspondence, 82, 125
Our Voice, 204
Over-stimulation. See Sensory overload

P

Panic attacks, 90
Parallel play, 146–147
    defined, 156, 209
Peer buddies, 48, 51, 96, 116, 124, 153, 175
    choosing, 139–140, 173
    defined, 209
    teaching, 140–141
People-first language, 50, 63, 209
Peppermint scents, 185
Perceptive communication, 209
Persistence, 176–177
Personal information
    helpful hints, 81
    teaching, 80–81
Personal space, 98, 140–141, 146–147, 165
    defined, 156, 209
Perspective sentences, 163
    defined, 178, 209
Pervasive Developmental Delay, 18–19
Photo albums, 131
Picture aprons. See Communication aprons
Picture cards, 62, 60, 69, 71, 77, 93, 97, 103, 108, 119–121, 125, 168
Picture cues, 126–127, 147, 149
Picture Exchange System, 120
Picture holders, 127
Picture schedules, 45, 53, 73, 78, 100, 120, 127
    defined, 209
    guidelines, 127
Picture sequence cards, 46, 69, 71, 77, 83, 99, 121, 137, 152

Pictures, 35, 116, 125–127, 152, 170
    children, 55, 174
    classroom tasks, 174
    clothing, 84
    coins, 82
    community helpers, 80
    depicting stop, 58
    family, 55
    of the child, 131
    pets, 55
    seasons, 84
    space aliens, 96
    using to communicate, 119–121
Pinching
    others, 31
    self, 29
Planning ahead, 201–202
Play, 16, 135–156
    choosing peer buddies, 139–140
    clean up, 154
    encouraging, 137–138
    games, 148–149, 151
    ideas, 141
    imaginative, 136–137, 156
    introducing toys, 142, 150
    joining in, 152–153
    observing, 138–139
    parallel, 146–147, 156
    pretend, 140–141, 156
    reciprocal, 136, 143, 156
    sharing, 144–145
    side-by-side, 145–147
    solitary, 137, 157
    stages, 136–137
    strategies, 143–155
    suggestions, 142
    symbolic, 136–137, 156
    teaching peer buddies, 140–141
    with props, 155
Pointing, 116
Portfolios, 37–38, 177
    defined, 41, 209
Positron Emission Tomography, 23
    defined, 26, 209
Pragmatic language, 109
    defined, 134, 209
Praise, 73, 77, 79, 85, 96, 99, 171, 177
Predictability, 66
Preparing other children, 61
Pretend play, 130, 136–137, 155
    defined, 156, 209
Prevalence of autism, 14
Proactive
    defined, 106, 209
    environment, 92
    strategies, 96

Problem solving, 35–36, 104, 131, 133, 170
   through play, 135
Proprioceptive sense, 186–187, 195
   defined, 196, 209
Puppets, 96, 130, 144
   using to communicate, 130
Putting on shoes/socks, 77
Puzzles, 144

Q
Quiet area, 29–30, 54, 97, 185

R
Reactive environment, 92
Receptive communication, 111
   defined, 134
Reciprocal communication, 114–116
Reciprocal play, 136, 143, 156, 209
Recorded music, 77, 99, 151, 193
Redirecting, 90, 98
Repeating phrases. See Echolalia
Repetitive actions, 19, 39, 137–138
Requesting communication, 113–114, 116
Resistance, 85, 95, 175
Respite care, 199, 205, 209
Rett's Syndome, 19–20
Reverse chaining, 77, 87, 209
Rhymes, 170–171
Ritualistic behaviors, 19, 26–28, 39, 41, 90, 209
   compulsive, 31
   disruptive, 31
   mealtime, 79
   reasons for, 30–31
Rocking, 28, 183
Role play, 86, 137, 155, 168
Routines, 19, 39, 45, 54, 132
   changes in, 100, 170, 175
   cleanup time, 154
   disruptions, 92
   hand washing, 83
   setting up, 46–47
   through life skills, 66
   toilet training, 73
Rules, 93, 149

S
Safety, 194–195
   personal information, 80–81
   traffic, 86
Sand, 186, 190, 192
Savants, 16
Scratching, 29, 183
Screaming, 89, 94, 113, 185
   function of, 91–93
   resistance, 95
   self-injurious, 27
   stereotypical, 19, 27

   strategies for coping, 90–91, 94–104
   understanding, 89–90
Security blankets, 30
See-n-Say toys, 144
Self-blame, 200
Self-calming, 173, 186–187, 193, 194–195
Self-care, 67, 72–86
Self-confidence, 159
Self-control, 159–160, 192
Self-esteem, 41, 57, 166–167, 176–177, 209
Self-injurious behaviors, 27–28, 90
   reasons for, 29–30
Self-stimulatory activities
   hand flapping, 142
   self-hitting, 142
Sensory integration, 179–196
   avoiding overload, 184–185
   detecting, 181–183
   helping, 184
   hidden senses, 185
   hypersensitivity, 182–183, 188, 190, 194–195
   hyposensitivity, 182–183, 186
   products for, 196
   seeing/hearing differently, 181
   SI Dysfunction, 180–181
   strategies, 186–195
   therapy, 22
Sensory Integration Disorder, 34–35, 41, 180–181, 196, 209
Sensory materials, 144
Sensory Modulation Disorder. See Sensory Integration Disorder
Sensory overload, 93, 102, 161, 194–195
   tantrums, 31
Sensory Resources, 196
Sensory stimuli responses, 15, 28
   explained, 34–35
Sentence starters, 132
Sequence cards. See Picture sequence cards
Serotonin, 26, 31, 290
Setting events, 91–92
   defined, 106, 209
Shapes, 188–189
Sharing, 144–145, 170
Shock, 199–200, 205
Shoe bags, 127
Signing, 33, 108, 113, 116, 118–119, 123–124, 129, 134, 141, 171
   feeding skills, 78
   signs, 126, 171, 119
   toilet training, 72
Singing, 128–129
Slapping, 31
Sleep issues, 92
Smells, 185
Snap-together toys, 144
Sniffing, 28, 183
Snuggle blankets, 187